THE BEDFORD SERIES IN HISTORY AND CULTURE

The Kitchen Debate and Cold War Consumer Politics

A Brief History with Documents

Related Titles in
THE BEDFORD SERIES IN HISTORY AND CULTURE
Advisory Editors: Lynn Hunt, *University of California, Los Angeles*
David W. Blight, *Yale University*
Bonnie G. Smith, *Rutgers University*
Natalie Zemon Davis, *University of Toronto*

THE BEDFORD SERIES IN HISTORY AND CULTURE

The Kitchen Debate and Cold War Consumer Politics

A Brief History with Documents

Shane Hamilton

University of Georgia

Sarah Phillips

Boston University

BEDFORD / ST. MARTIN'S   Boston   ◆   New York

For Bedford/St. Martin's

Publisher for History: Mary V. Dougherty
Senior Executive Editor for History and Technology: William J. Lombardo
Director of Development for History: Jane Knetzger
Executive Editor: Elizabeth M. Welch
Publishing Services Manager: Andrea Cava
Senior Production Supervisor: Steven Cestaro
Executive Marketing Manager: Sandra McGuire
Editorial Assistant: Laura Kintz
Project Management: Books By Design, Inc.
Senior Art Director: Anna Palchik
Text Design: Claire Seng-Niemoeller
Cover Design: Marine Miller
Cover Photo: Time & Life Pictures/Getty Images
Composition: Achorn International, Inc.
Printing and Binding: RR Donnelley and Sons

President, Bedford/St. Martin's: Denise B. Wydra
Director of Marketing: Karen R. Soeltz
Production Director: Susan W. Brown
Director of Rights and Permissions: Hilary Newman

Manufactured in the United States of America.

8   7   6   5   4   3
f   e   d   c   b   a

For information, write: Bedford / St. Martin's, 75 Arlington Street, Boston, MA 02116
(617-399-4000)

ISBN 978-0-312-67710-7

Acknowledgments

Acknowledgments and copyrights are continued at the back of the book on pages 161–62, which constitute an extension of the copyright page. It is a violation of the law to reproduce these selections by any means whatsoever without the written permission of the copyright holder.

About the cover: Soviet premier Nikita Khrushchev and U.S. vice president Richard Nixon beside a model kitchen display at the American National Exhibition in Moscow, July 1, 1959.

Foreword

The Bedford Series in History and Culture is designed so that readers can study the past as historians do.

The historian's first task is finding the evidence. Documents, letters, memoirs, interviews, pictures, movies, novels, or poems can provide facts and clues. Then the historian questions and compares the sources. There is more to do than in a courtroom, for hearsay evidence is welcome, and the historian is usually looking for answers beyond act and motive. Different views of an event may be as important as a single verdict. How a story is told may yield as much information as what it says.

Along the way the historian seeks help from other historians and perhaps from specialists in other disciplines. Finally, it is time to write, to decide on an interpretation and how to arrange the evidence for readers.

Each book in this series contains an important historical document or group of documents, each document a witness from the past and open to interpretation in different ways. The documents are combined with some element of historical narrative—an introduction or a biographical essay, for example—that provides students with an analysis of the primary source material and important background information about the world in which it was produced.

Each book in the series focuses on a specific topic within a specific historical period. Each provides a basis for lively thought and discussion about several aspects of the topic and the historian's role. Each is short enough (and inexpensive enough) to be a reasonable one-week assignment in a college course. Whether as classroom or personal reading, each book in the series provides firsthand experience of the challenge—and fun—of discovering, recreating, and interpreting the past.

Lynn Hunt
David W. Blight
Bonnie G. Smith
Natalie Zemon Davis

For Bea and Clem, Finley and Iris. —SP and SH

Preface

The Kitchen Debate is rightly understood as a defining moment of the cold war. When, in 1959, U.S. vice president Richard Nixon and Soviet premier Nikita Khrushchev traded barbs in a bright yellow kitchen display at the American National Exhibition in Moscow, their exchange illuminated the deep ideological and cultural divide between the two superpowers. Students are often exposed to the military and diplomatic rivalries of the cold war period. This book uses the Kitchen Debate to illustrate the cold war as a vocal and hotly contested battle over living standards. Both U.S. and Soviet leaders understood the usefulness of kitchens as weapons—perhaps more powerful than even nuclear bombs—in a war that was fought over the terrain of political economy, culture, and consumer desires.

The Kitchen Debate and Cold War Consumer Politics is intended to meet the need for a short, document-based book that combines the domestic and international facets of the cold war. The Introduction lays out three key themes that resonate throughout the book: the consensus politics of the "American way of life" as contrasted to the Soviet state-run economy in the 1950s and 1960s; the ideology of "redomestication," which restructured gender relations during the era of containment; and the global politics of food during the height of the cold war. The primary documents that make up the core of the book have been selected to illustrate each of these themes in depth. The widely varying selections—ranging from government documents, newspaper reports, and archival records to cartoons and photographs—allow students to explore history as professional historians do. Many of the selections represent U.S. viewpoints, but we include a number of documents translated from Russian so students can see the Kitchen Debate from the perspective of Soviet leaders and citizens as well.

Although the Kitchen Debate has long been recognized as a key event in the cold war, this is the first source collection to use it to interweave the domestic culture and global politics of the cold war era. The

documents illustrate that the Kitchen Debate was not a single brief episode, but in fact took place over several days and in multiple locations.
Both world leaders delivered scripted speeches as well as impromptu
remarks, and this volume provides carefully selected transcripts of the
most significant discussions. We also include selections on farm and
food policy to provide an unexpected, yet illuminating, window onto
the domestic and global reach of cold war consumer culture and the
international rivalry over living standards. Few students, for example,
understand that after World War II American agriculture underwent
the largest, fastest, and most sustained industrial revolution in world
history—a revolution closely watched in the Soviet Union. An industri-
alizing farmscape produced enormous quantities of inexpensive food,
bolstering middle-class Americans' views of themselves as a "people of
plenty" in a supposedly classless society. This book puts such issues
into historical context, exploring the rise of the supermarket and the
TV dinner, Soviet efforts to boost meat and milk production, and the
deployment of international food assistance. Food, in short, provided an
overarching framework for superpower competition, as well as an arena
for a shared analysis of national strength.

To aid students' analysis of the selections, each document opens with
a headnote that provides essential background, and explanatory foot-
notes clarify the events described. At the end of the book, students and
instructors will find a chronology that places the Kitchen Debate in historical context, a list of questions suitable for discussion or for writing
assignments, and a selected bibliography with suggestions for further
reading.

ACKNOWLEDGMENTS

A number of people helped us with this book. We thank William J. Lombardo, senior executive editor for history at Bedford/St. Martin's, for
seeking us out, and David Blight, advisory editor for the Bedford Series
in History and Culture, for supporting this volume. For their help with
the project, we thank Mary Dougherty, Heidi Hood, Andrea Cava, and
Nancy Benjamin. Most important, we acknowledge the superb guidance from executive editor Elizabeth M. Welch and the assistance of
Laura Kintz.

The reviewers whose comments helped us shape the final manu-
script deserve our gratitude: Jeffrey Bass, Arizona State University; M.
Todd Bennett, East Carolina University; Steven J. Bucklin, University of

South Dakota; David Engerman, Brandeis University; Michael Flamm, Ohio Wesleyan University; and Sheyda Jahanbani, Kansas University.

A very special thanks is due to Charles Byrd, expert in Russian language and culture, for his translations and guidance on the following documents: Document 34, R. Podol'nyi, "Technology on the March"; Document 35, Marietta Shaginian, "Reflections on the American Exhibition"; and Document 36, I. Luchkova and A. Sikachev, "Is There a Science of the Home?"

Shane Hamilton
Sarah Phillips

Contents

Illustrations

THE BEDFORD SERIES IN HISTORY AND CULTURE

The Kitchen Debate and Cold War Consumer Politics

A Brief History with Documents

PART ONE

Introduction: The Kitchen Debate in Historical Context

In late July 1959, U.S. Vice President Richard Nixon arrived in Moscow to open the American National Exhibition. The carefully staged six-week exhibit in Moscow's suburban Sokolniki Park, Nixon declared, would provide Soviet citizens "a clearer picture of life in the United States."[1] That "clearer picture" included an astonishing display of the abundance available to American consumers: mass-produced automobiles, color televisions, ranch-style suburban homes. At the heart of the exhibition were several model kitchens stocked with technological gadgetry and modern convenience foods. The kitchens in Sokolniki Park soon became famous the world over as the backdrop for what journalists dubbed the "Kitchen Debate." In one of the most emblematic exchanges of the cold war era, Nixon and Soviet Premier Nikita Khrushchev waged a war of words over the respective merits of socialism and capitalism (see Documents 5 and 6). The Kitchen Debate, centered on the politics and culture of mass consumption, revealed that the cold war was not just a geopolitical confrontation between two nuclear-armed superpowers. It was also a battle for the hearts, the minds, and—perhaps most importantly—the stomachs of citizens in the cold war world.

Soviet visitors to the American National Exhibition in Moscow paid a mere ruble to witness a spectacular display of U.S. economic productivity. Looming over the entrance to the ten-acre pavilion was a space-age, gold-plated geodesic dome. Inside the dome, seven giant screens flashed thousands of images of Americans working, playing, shopping

1

at supermarkets, and driving on interstate highways. Leaving the dome, visitors proceeded to a fifty-thousand-square-foot glass pavilion stuffed from floor to ceiling with American consumer goods. Modern furniture, color televisions, dishwashers, vacuum cleaners, wedding dresses, lipstick tubes, plastic wares, gleaming pots and pans—all of these consumer items and many more were dangled before Soviet citizens as "proof of national grandeur" in what one historian has called a "combat of commodities."[2]

Several kitchens prominently displayed in the glass pavilion formed the centerpiece of this consumer propaganda campaign. An RCA/Whirlpool "Miracle Kitchen" provided a glimpse of an imagined future of drudgery-free housework: A robotic floor cleaner and an automated push-button "planning center" would bring the homemaker into the computer age. In another kitchen, home economists demonstrated ready-made cake mixes and frozen foods (see Documents 9 and 10). A small but up-to-date model of an apartment-style American kitchen stood nearby. Other exhibits on display in Sokolniki Park included chrome-laden automobiles, a booth providing free samples of Pepsi-Cola, an IBM RAMAC computer programmed to tout the American way of life, a 360° Circarama movie by Walt Disney, and a prefabricated ranch-style home. Inside the model suburban home was yet another kitchen, sponsored by General Electric. Here, over the six weeks of the exhibition, more than two and a half million Soviet visitors saw firsthand an array of appliances portrayed as essential markers of middle-class status: a dishwasher, garbage disposal, countertop cooking range, and combination refrigerator-freezer.[3] It was in this canary-yellow kitchen that Nixon, pulling Khrushchev close, announced, "I want to show you this kitchen," initiating one of the most memorable diplomatic encounters of the cold war.

THE COLD WAR, CONTAINMENT, AND "PEACEFUL COMPETITION"

Few observers would have predicted this jovial exchange in summertime Moscow, given the tense history of relations between the United States and the Soviet Union. The Bolshevik Revolution of 1917 and the formal establishment of the Soviet Union as a communist[4] state in 1922 sparked decades of hostility between East and West. After the Soviet Union's first leader, Vladimir Lenin, died in 1924, his successor, Joseph Stalin, developed a policy of "socialism in one country," intending to strengthen his own nation rather than foment a worldwide revolution of the working classes. Nonetheless, Stalin remained convinced that Western powers were permanently hostile to the USSR's existence. Stalin was correct, in part, as most Americans in the twentieth century viewed the world through Wilsonian lenses. In 1918, President Woodrow Wilson issued a blueprint for a new post–World War I international order. The principles he put forth, known as the Fourteen Points, held that all the world's people would experience freedom and prosperity as they secured rights to national self-determination and opened their markets to overseas trade and investment. These Wilsonian assumptions clashed with an equally universalist worldview on the Soviet side, which held that class struggle drove history forward and that socialism would replace capitalism worldwide. Because these incompatible ideologies concretely shaped the two nations' foreign policies, persistent conflict of some sort was inevitable.[5]

But the cold war—the overt military standoff and global competition between the United States and the Soviet Union from 1947 to 1991—was not simply rooted in the inevitable clash of irreconcilable ideologies.[6] It also emerged from the specific context of World War II (1937–1945), in which the United States and the Soviet Union fought together to defeat Nazi Germany. Both parties viewed the wartime arrangement as a marriage of convenience, and both Franklin Roosevelt and Joseph Stalin predicted a certain measure of power sharing after the hostilities ended. The question was how that would happen.

Stalin's overriding concern was the security of his western border. The war with Germany had claimed the lives of millions of Soviet citizens, the Soviet economic base was devastated, and Stalin expected territory and resources to make up for his country's sacrifices. Stalin also believed that the United States and Great Britain had agreed to the future Soviet dominance of much of eastern and southeastern Europe. Unlike Stalin, though, the American president who succeeded Roosevelt in 1945—Harry Truman—had to answer to American constituents who watched in horror as the Soviets installed communist governments in the East from 1945 to 1948. Within central Europe, Germany's fate alone still rested in the hands of both powers. Though forces from all the Allied countries occupied Germany after the war, Stalin had made it plain that he intended to strip the Soviet zone of its assets and resources. The Americans and the British, however, understood that economic recovery for Europe hinged on a rebuilt Germany. No settlement of the German question was possible without agreement between the United States and the Soviet Union on the future of Europe as a whole—a profoundly unlikely event that showcased how the outcome of World

War II provided a specific battleground for the two powers' irreconcilable interests.

Thus, within the span of just a few years, the United States and the Soviet Union moved from wartime allies to bitter rivals. In the war's aftermath, the United States also launched its enduring foreign-policy approach to the Soviet Union: the strategy of containment. Arising from the ideas of diplomat George F. Kennan, who had observed Soviet behavior from a post in Moscow and attempted to explain it in the increasingly hostile atmosphere of 1946 and 1947, containment's main premise was that relations with the Soviet Union could never proceed on a basis of mutual trust. The foreign policy of the Soviet Union was, according to Kennan, inevitably driven by paranoia. Moreover, diplomacy and honest engagement would not deter Soviet expansionism; Stalin, in particular, seemed to have designs on much more than Eastern Europe. "Soviet policies will reflect no abstract love of peace and stability, no real faith in the possibility of a permanent happy coexistence of the Socialist and capitalist worlds," Kennan argued, "but rather a cautious, persistent pressure towards the disruption and weakening of all rival influence and power."[7]

Truman put Kennan's ideas of containment into practice, drawing a line beyond which Soviet expansion would not be tolerated even as the United States made no attempt to liberate Eastern European areas already in the Soviet sphere. The Truman Doctrine of 1947 provided the first formal statement of containment policy when Truman announced moral and financial support for anticommunist forces in Greece and Turkey. Framing the action in sweeping terms, Truman declared his intent to "support free peoples who are resisting attempted subjugation by armed minorities or by outside pressures."[8] Containing communist influence in Europe, without the direct use of military force against the Soviet Union, was now official U.S. policy. The cold war had begun.

The Truman Doctrine marked a major turning point in American history: Presidents henceforth deployed fear to obtain domestic support for cold war foreign policy.[9] Truman also used the doctrine's reasoning to justify the 1948 Marshall Plan, an enormous multibillion-dollar program to assist and rebuild postwar Europe. The North Atlantic Treaty Organization (NATO), a mutual defense pact among the United States and the countries of Western Europe, followed quickly on the heels of the Marshall Plan in 1949. The United States now committed itself to a permanent military presence in Western Europe.[10] With the Molotov Plan (1947) and the Warsaw Pact (1955), Stalin likewise knit together Eastern European satellites into an economic and military empire. When

Stalin closed off roads, rail lines, electricity, and communications to West Berlin in 1948 (the Soviets controlled only the eastern portion of the former capital of Germany), Truman ordered an airlift of food and supplies. Nearly a year passed before the Soviets lifted the blockade. Truman had scored a victory over Stalin, withstanding the first major challenge to the policy of containment without starting a new war. The cost was high, however, as Germany and its capital—indeed, all of Europe—would remain divided between East and West until 1989.

Nuclear weapons, like the policy of containment, helped ensure that the cold war would be long-lived, complex, and costly. The U.S. nuclear bombs that destroyed the Japanese cities of Hiroshima and Nagasaki in 1945 were the first and last atomic weapons used in warfare. For a few years after the end of World War II, the United States maintained a monopoly on atomic weapons. American hopes that the United States might retain this advantage for another decade were dashed in August 1949 when the USSR tested its first atomic bomb. Stalin, in fact, launched a massive armament program after hearing the news of Hiroshima, enlisting most of the nation's scarce industrial and financial resources in the quest. Indeed, the Soviet nuclear program helped establish a persistent pattern in the country's postwar planning: Industry and weapons came first, the civilian economy second. It also marked the beginning of a decades-long nuclear arms race, as each country built more and more powerful atomic weapons, including hydrogen bombs and intercontinental ballistic missiles capable of delivering warheads across oceans. By the mid-1950s, each nation had enough nuclear weaponry to obliterate the other. As a result, one of the defining strategies of the cold war was the principle of mutual assured destruction (MAD): Both sides understood that a nuclear attack would be sheer madness, as it would precipitate a devastating return volley. Both nations thus had reason to pursue ways of engaging the enemy without resorting to direct military attack.

Opportunities for indirect engagement emerged most dramatically in Asia in the 1950s. Through 1948 the cold war had remained primarily a European conflict, but the Chinese Revolution of 1949, under the communist leadership of Mao Zedong, shifted attention to a vast region of the world where the end of World War II had also left in place a power vacuum. While Mao operated independently of Stalin, Americans fretted that the communist world had nearly doubled overnight—and that Moscow was leading the charge. Thus when North Korean forces poured into South Korea in 1950, over the dividing line that separated the postwar occupation zones of the Soviet Union and the United States, the United States sent forces to beat back the communist advance. During the Korean War, the Americans attempted to wrest control of the entire peninsula and fought directly with Chinese forces in this ultimately unsuccessful gamble. Although a formal peace was never declared in the Korean War, hostilities ceased with an armistice in 1953. This was the first and only conflict of the cold war in which U.S. soldiers squared off directly against one of the two major communist world powers. After Korea, the cold war across Asia—and the globe—would take the shape of proxy wars in places like Vietnam, Afghanistan, and Guatemala, with the Americans and Soviets choosing sides and supplying their clients with money and materials.

Truman had initiated the policy of containment; his successor, Dwight Eisenhower, adapted it for an increasingly global conflict. Eisenhower also extended and prioritized another strategy: psychological warfare. During the 1950s, the United States pursued an all-out war of ideas, using cultural diplomacy and semisecret propaganda campaigns in an effort to "win" the cold war by convincing the world's citizens that only democracy and capitalism could ensure material comfort and political freedoms. Appealing to "the common man's yearning for food, shelter, and a decent standard of living" would, Eisenhower assured a team of foreign policy advisers in 1953, ultimately secure victory for the United States.[11] The key institution for promoting this "soft power" agenda was the U.S. Information Agency (USIA), a propaganda machine created by Eisenhower in 1953. Over the course of the 1950s, the USIA worked with private American corporations to advertise the "American way of life" to world audiences, showing off supermarkets, station wagons, and model American homes in countries throughout the world.[12] Thus even as Eisenhower formally declared his commitment to the policy of containment, the United States wielded ideological weapons in an effort to undermine communist regimes.

The conviction that the USSR would take every opportunity to expand its influence and power also extended to the domestic sphere. The Soviets, as Kennan avowed in an internal telegram in 1946, strove on a "subterranean plane" to "disrupt national self-confidence," "hamstring measures of national defense," and "increase social and industrial unrest."[13] Many Americans embraced this reasoning and believed that Soviet agents were at work inside the United States, destabilizing the country's foreign policy and weakening its national resolve. Between 1950 and 1954, Wisconsin Senator Joseph McCarthy preyed on such fears of domestic subversion. With a suite of tactics despised by critics as "McCarthyism," the senator accused the federal government of harboring communists and publicly questioned the political beliefs of thousands of Americans from government officials to Hollywood film-makers to ordinary schoolteachers.

McCarthy was not the first to whip up anticommunist hysteria, however, as attempts to discredit leftist political beliefs began well before McCarthy's time and permeated all levels of government as well as the nation's private institutions.[14] Fears of communist infiltration were not totally unfounded. A few Americans secretly passed sensitive information to the Soviets during World War II. But years of aggressive federal persecution of former communists and suspected communist sympathizers meant that, by the time of McCarthy's accusations, spy rings and the Communist Party U.S.A. had largely folded.[15] While investigators exposed a few cases of atomic espionage and political disloyalty, these revelations were eclipsed by the pernicious results of the post–World War II Red Scare: Mere dissent became supposed disloyalty, thousands of innocents lost their jobs, and political freedoms were suppressed at home even as the United States undertook to promote liberty abroad.

The anxious atmosphere of the era meant that a savvy politician could take advantage of the anticommunist fervor to advance his career. No politician better exploited that opportunity than Richard Nixon (1913–1994). A native Californian, Nixon grew up working long hours at his father's small gas and grocery store. He excelled at debate, attended a local college, and graduated third in his class from Duke Law School. That rank, however, was not enough to earn him an offer from a top law firm — an insult that shaped Nixon's lifelong resentment of the East Coast liberal establishment. In 1946, a group of California businessmen backed him for a Congressional seat, and Nixon craftily "Red-baited" the incumbent, calling him more "Communistic than Democratic." Once elected, Nixon helped expose Alger Hiss, an Ivy League–educated Democrat who had attempted to conceal his role as a Soviet informant during World War II. Nixon's success in painting liberal elites as communist sympathizers secured him a national profile, and in 1950 he ascended to the Senate. Moscow, Nixon said, was ready to call on its hidden allies inside the United States to start a "reign of terror" if the United States crossed swords with Russia: "If You Want to Work for Uncle Sam Instead of Slave for Uncle Joe, Vote for Richard Nixon."[16] Despite his extreme, even conspiratorial, anticommunist rhetoric, Nixon's internationalist approach to foreign policy put him at the ideological center of the Republican Party. He believed in a strong role for the United States in NATO and supported the Marshall Plan. His dynamic approach to conservative politics garnered Nixon the vice presidency under Eisenhower from 1953 to 1961.

In the Soviet Union, meanwhile, dramatic political transformations shaped the course of the cold war. Joseph Stalin died in March 1953. An intense battle to replace him ensued, with Nikita Khrushchev (1894–1971) ultimately emerging as the victor. The son of poor peasants, Khrushchev transitioned from factory work to politics in the aftermath of the Bolshevik Revolution. Through the 1920s and 1930s, Khrushchev worked his way rapidly up the Communist Party ranks, becoming the leader of the Moscow Party organization and overseer of the construction of the Moscow Metro, an underground rail system that opened in 1935 to great public fanfare. Khrushchev ingratiated himself with Stalin, even assisting in the purges of the mid-1930s in which thousands of Stalin's supposed political enemies suffered persecution, exile, and execution. Through World War II and into the early 1950s, Khrushchev solidified his place in Stalin's inner circle, but few observers expected him to ascend to the head of the Soviet Communist Party. Shortly after Stalin's death, however, Khrushchev consolidated his power by cultivating allies, proposing bold domestic reforms, and undermining rivals. By 1955, he pushed his last major opponents off stage and became the undisputed leader of the Soviet Union.[17]

Khrushchev's rise to power brought possibilities for better relations with the West. He attended an international peace conference at Geneva and met with Eisenhower in 1955. In a February 1956 "secret speech," Khrushchev denounced the brutal tactics and dictatorial rule of his predecessor, and he weathered severe attacks from Kremlin rivals for doing so. Yet Khrushchev's approach to foreign policy was unpredictable and often confounding. Before a group of Western diplomats in 1956, Khrushchev bluntly announced, "We will bury you!"[18] Americans took the statement as a veiled nuclear threat, but Khrushchev had simply meant to convey a standard communist conviction that socialism was destined to outlive capitalism. Later in 1956, a series of crises brought new challenges to Khrushchev's foreign policy goals. Workers in Soviet-controlled Poland mounted a mass strike to demand "bread and freedom," and Hungarians rose up in mass revolt against Kremlin control. Soviet armed forces crushed both uprisings to keep the Eastern Bloc countries firmly in the Soviet sphere.

Seeking to solidify his political legitimacy abroad and at home, Khrushchev declared his intent to pursue a policy of "peaceful coexistence" with the West. Few Americans took Khrushchev's apparent softening of tone very seriously at first, particularly after the Soviets launched the *Sputnik I* satellite in October 1957, igniting fears of a space war. In November 1958, a year after the satellite's launch, Khrushchev further aggravated western diplomats with his "Berlin ultimatum," proposing to sign a formal peace treaty with East Germany and to cut off the divided capital of Berlin permanently from the West. When the Soviet leadership backed down from the ultimatum in May 1959, however, icy relations between the two superpowers thawed briefly. Although Khrushchev would later reignite tensions with the West, particularly with the construction of the Berlin Wall in 1961 and during the Cuban Missile Crisis of 1962, a window opened in the summer of 1959 for a very different kind of cold war standoff.

Meeting at the American National Exhibition in Moscow in July, Nixon and Khrushchev took advantage of the reduction in tensions and avoided a thorough public airing of diplomatic grievances. They focused instead on what Khrushchev called "peaceful competition," with each leader boasting of his country's ability to deliver high standards of living, affordable homes, and laborsaving appliances. While Khrushchev was keen to point out that Americans, unlike Soviet citizens, held no right to housing, Nixon quickly parried that Americans chose diversity in their consumer options and did not wish "to have one decision made at the top by one government official." Nixon touted the range of goods available to American consumers, but Khrushchev dismissed American lemon squeezers and lawn mowers as "merely gadgets." Nixon insisted that American technologies "make easier the life of our housewives," while Khrushchev attacked the American "capitalist attitude toward women" (see Document 5).

Despite the often playful tone of the two leaders' sparring, the issues addressed during the Kitchen Debate were of utmost seriousness. For U.S. and Soviet leaders, the American kitchens in Moscow — and the consumer abundance they symbolized — served as one of the most important battlegrounds in the cold war. Unable to deploy nuclear weapons against each other for fear of mutual assured destruction, the two superpowers instead waged war in the realm of consumer expectations and desires.

From the perspective of the U.S. officials who planned the American National Exhibition, the gleaming kitchens in Sokolniki Park were intended to serve as material proof of the superiority of capitalism over socialism. Indeed, planners in the USIA viewed the kitchens in Moscow as weapons in the ongoing cold war battle of ideas. A government document laying out the basic goals for the American National Exhibition distinguished between the exhibit's publicly stated objective and its supposedly secret mission. Publicly, the USIA touted the exhibit as a goodwill gesture aimed at educating Soviet people about American life.

Privately, the exhibit's planners expected the displays to make Soviet visitors dissatisfied with their economic circumstances and with Communist Party rule. The kitchens staged in Sokolniki Park in 1959 were thus part of an ongoing Eisenhower administration campaign to wage a psychological cold war centered on consumer desires for the good life (see Documents 1–4 and 12).

Soviet leaders were quick to expose the propagandistic nature of the American National Exhibit, but they, too, had ample reason to see kitchens as crucial battlegrounds in the cold war (see Document 11). "The kitchen," one historian has argued, "was a central site for the linked projects of modernization and advanced construction of communism in the Cold War context of 'peaceful competition.'"[19] Especially for Soviet Premier Nikita Khrushchev, the kitchen was much more than a symbol of consumption. It was the place where Soviet citizens consumed the most important product of the socialist economy: food. In his first speech as Communist Party secretary in 1953, Khrushchev called on Soviet leaders to find a "solution of the task of creating an abundance of consumers' goods in our country." The place to start, Khrushchev announced, was to rapidly boost Soviet agricultural production, particularly to provision the meat, dairy, and fresh produce increasingly demanded by the nation's populace.[20] From that speech onward, Khrushchev staked his regime on promises of plenty. As he said in 1955, "The people put it to us this way: Will there be meat to eat, or not? Will there be milk, or not? Will there be decent pairs of pants? This isn't ideology, of course, but what good does it do if everyone is ideologically correct but goes around without trousers?"[21] Emphasizing agricultural production and consumer goods manufacturing alongside heavy industry, Khrushchev declared, would do more than create a satisfied Soviet populace. It would propel the Soviet Union past the United States as the most productive economy on the planet. When Khrushchev informed Nixon during the Kitchen Debate that the USSR would soon "be on the same level as America," his grin belied the gravity of his declaration that "while passing by we will wave back to you."[22]

In early 1957, the Soviet Union launched its most important offensive in this regard, a campaign to outproduce American farmers. In May 1957, Khrushchev pledged to a conference of agricultural workers that the Soviet Union would, "in the next few years," overtake the United States in per capita output of meat, butter, and milk. "This victory of ours," Khrushchev announced to thundering applause, "will be stronger than the hydrogen bomb."[23] Well-provisioned communist kitchens were, for Khrushchev, crucial for maintaining his political legitimacy both in the international realm and in domestic Soviet politics.

American journalists half-mockingly dubbed the July 1959 joust between Nixon and Khrushchev the "Kitchen Debate," implying that discussions of garbage disposals and dishwashers were not really the stuff of superpower diplomacy (see Document 16). But their mockery belied an important truth. Central to Richard Nixon's tribute to the abundance of postwar American consumer society was the suburban kitchen itself—the laborsaving dishwashers and washing machines, the inexpensive supermarket groceries delivered from scientifically sophisticated farms, and family meals prepared by American house-wives. Khrushchev may have scoffed at the futuristic "Miracle Kitchen" in Sokolniki Park, but he held a deep reverence for the American model of industrial agriculture that provided the abundance he knew was available in actual middle-class American kitchens. Indeed, Khrushchev revived the central themes of the Kitchen Debate in September 1959 when he visited the United States. Touring the cornfields of Iowa, the Soviet leader waxed poetic on the technological and scientific sophistication of American farms. He tasted his first hot dog. He visited an American supermarket. And he declared once again that his socialist nation would shortly overtake the United States in the production of food. The economic contest between the capitalist West and the communist East, it seemed, would be waged primarily in the kitchens and agricultural fields of the world's mighty superpowers. Three key lines of battle were mapped out at the Kitchen Debate: the role of government in shaping economic abundance, the role of women in modern society, and the global politics of food production and consumption.

THE POLITICS OF ABUNDANCE

The American Exhibition in Moscow was designed to demonstrate the "American way of life" to the Soviet masses. The exhibition's focus on typical household goods, meant to represent the average American lifestyle, upheld a vision of a homogenous, affluent America. The booming post–World War II economy brought unprecedented prosperity to blue-collar industrial workers. Americans' faith in capitalism, sorely tested during the Great Depression of the 1930s, was quickly restored in the war's aftermath. The U.S. government, in fact, took an active hand in restoring and maintaining economic prosperity. Yet the perceived threat of the Soviet Union's authoritarian rule and command economy, in which every important economic decision was dictated by Soviet planners, ensured that both liberals and conservatives in the United States held to a consensus vision that tied economic abundance with mass

consumption. Republicans and Democrats disagreed on the specifics
of tax policy, government spending, support for organized labor, and
international trade, but they agreed that the government's primary role
in the economy was to support mass consumption and to ensure the
stability of markets dominated by large corporations.

World War II ended the privation of the Great Depression. U.S. entry
into the war meant that an enormous army had to be built essentially
from scratch. Industrial manpower had to be mobilized to produce the
needed airplanes, ships, tanks, guns, and bombs. The ways in which the
federal government erected this "arsenal of democracy" had important
effects for big business and for organized labor. For big business, the
war created opportunities for major industrial corporations to expand
their output in ways that had not been possible since the U.S. stock
market crash of 1929. Massive government spending during the war
was funneled to large private corporations: The fifty-six largest corporations in America received three-quarters of wartime defense contracts.
Organized labor also benefitted. During World War II, the organized
labor movement cemented its place in the American economy. Between
1941 and 1945, union membership rose from 10.5 million to 14.75 million, encouraged in part by the National War Labor Board's support of
unionized labor in exchange for a "no-strike pledge" and in part by an
increasingly militant stance among rank-and-file union members who
demanded wage and benefit increases during the war. The wartime successes of labor unions paid off handsomely, as the per capita income of
blue-collar workers increased faster than that of white-collar workers for
the first time in American history.

Emboldened by this newfound prosperity, President Franklin Roosevelt and the Democratic Party insisted that World War II was not just
about defeating fascists overseas. Indeed, Roosevelt tapped into a growing sense among many Americans that the war's end would open up new
forms of economic citizenship. Speaking before Congress in one of his
most famous wartime addresses, the 1941 State of the Union Address,
Roosevelt described a new world order after the war, in which four
"essential human freedoms" would reign: freedom of speech, freedom from fear, freedom of worship, and freedom from want. Roosevelt
repeatedly referred to these four freedoms throughout the war, uphold-
ing the ideas as embodiments of traditional American values. But the
notion of "freedom from want" was a remarkable declaration of a not-so-
traditional idea. The phrase implied that the power of American capitalism, guided by an active federal government, could provide the "good
life" to *all* American citizens. By the end of the war, Roosevelt linked

this notion of "freedom from want" to an economic goal of protecting the future standard of living of American workers by guaranteeing that the Depression would not resume after the war. This, Roosevelt declared, would bring "real freedom for the common man."[24]

Prosperity was indeed remarkably widespread for average Americans after World War II. U.S. output of goods and services doubled between 1946 and 1956, and it would double again by 1970. Between 1949 and 1973, median family income doubled, even when adjusted for inflation. With higher incomes, Americans spent more money, especially on consumer durable goods. Household appliances and furnishings were sold to the tune of billions of dollars. Electric refrigerators, washing machines, and televisions—all quite rare before the war—became standard features in postwar homes. Automobile sales boomed, too. Sales of new cars quadrupled between 1946 and 1955. By 1960, three-fourths of American households owned at least one car, and automobiles outnumbered families in the nation. Also by 1960, with generous federal backing of home mortgages via the Federal Housing Administration and the Veterans Administration, two out of three American families were able to buy their own homes.

Widespread demand for appliances, cars, and houses ensured that even workers with limited education could obtain good-paying factory and construction jobs. Blue-collar industrial workers who belonged to unions enjoyed high wages, steady employment, and impressive benefits packages. Public intellectuals began celebrating a supposedly "classless" society. Russell Lynes, author of an influential 1949 essay titled "High-Brow, Low-Brow, Middle-Brow," declared that economic class was "obsolete" in America, with the only important distinctions in U.S. society defined by cultural taste and individual choice. Sociologist William Whyte likewise declared culture and taste to be more significant dividing lines than economic class, a line of thought further pursued by popular writer Vance Packard in his best-selling 1959 study, *The Status Seekers*. Such writers suggested that the economic antagonisms that had so animated U.S. political culture during the Great Depression had now vanished, replaced by contests of culture.[25]

Mass consumption was widely recognized as the engine driving postwar America's economic growth. Owing to his promotion of government strategies to boost demand for goods and services, British economist John Maynard Keynes became one of the most influential thinkers in American politics after the war. There was a certain irony in the postwar adoption of Keynes's liberal view that, in times of economic crisis, governments need to boost their spending to compensate for weak consumer demand. Keynes had promoted this notion of "compensatory spending" as a solution to the Great Depression in the 1930s, but most Americans—including Franklin Roosevelt—remained deeply skeptical that debt-fueled government spending could do anything other than drive the federal budget into the red. Massive government spending during the war validated Keynesian economics, however, as government outlays boosted industrial production, revived consumer confidence, and put people back to work. After the war, both Democratic and Republican politicians accepted the notion that government spending and tax policies could foster mass consumption, redistribute wealth into the hands of working Americans, boost corporate profits, and expand the economic pie. Indeed, the private act of consumption was widely understood in the postwar period to be a public duty, essential for the national interest[26] (see Document 20). Buying a new Ford or Chrysler loaded with options may have satisfied a buyer's desire for a nice ride, but from the perspective of Keynesian economic thinkers, it more importantly ensured that workers would have good-paying jobs in the automobile industry, fueling an ever-expanding economy driven by the logic of mass consumption.

For all the celebratory rhetoric of mass consumption, this liberal economic consensus had deep cracks (see Document 21). Conservatives drew on continuing antigovernment sentiment in postwar America, suggesting that government spending and regulation of businesses were forms of "creeping socialism." Richard Nixon, who staked his early political career on such conflations of liberalism with socialism, attacked the Democratic Party's support for the postwar continuation of wartime price controls. Foreshadowing his 1959 performance in Moscow, Nixon piled up kitchen appliances in his campaign office in 1946 to prove that an abundance of consumer goods existed, if only liberals would unshackle American businesses from the profit-dampening effects of price controls.[27] When a Republican-led congressional coalition successfully forced the end of price controls in 1946, it set the stage for waves of modest yet persistent inflation in the postwar era that weakened the liberal coalition of organized labor, middle-class consumers, Democratic policymakers, and progressive business leaders. Many business owners and members of the white-collar middle class came to resent the power of organized labor in the late 1940s and 1950s, seeing workers' wage increases as contributing to a "wage-price spiral" that drove up the cost of goods. Conservative politicians tapped into this sentiment to successfully push legislation, such as the 1947 Taft-Hartley Act, intended to roll back the strength of labor unions.[28]

Perhaps most importantly, even if expanding mass consumption seemed to be creating a "classless" society, racial inequality remained a primary fissure in postwar America. The federal policies of the 1930s and 1940s that created the postwar middle class—minimum wage legislation and union recognition, retirement pensions, home mortgages, and college educations—largely bypassed African Americans in a process that one scholar has memorably labeled "affirmative action for whites."[29] When Martin Luther King Jr. visited an Alabama cotton farm in 1965, he was shocked to meet black sharecroppers who had never seen a U.S. dollar bill in their lives, having been paid only in locally redeemable scrip for their backbreaking labor. Even affluent African Americans faced rampant discrimination when they attempted to buy into the suburban good life after World War II, as federal housing policies and white homeowners' fears of neighborhoods "going bad" due to racial mixing ensured that the postwar flight to the suburbs would be racially stratified. While the civil rights movement scored impressive successes in challenging the legal bases of Jim Crow segregation in the mid-1950s, the specter of economic disfranchisement would haunt black leaders and tug at the nation's conscience for decades to come. It is no accident that many of the historic events of the civil rights movement—the 1955 Montgomery bus boycott, the 1960 Greensboro Woolworth's sit-in, the 1961 Freedom Rides—were predicated on demonstrating the buying power of African Americans and the bad economics of maintaining segregation. For many black citizens, as well as for many Hispanics and Native Americans, the American dream of upward mobility and economic security was more fiction than reality in the 1950s and 1960s.

The cold war threat of the Soviet Union, however, provided the essential glue that held the postwar liberal economic consensus together in those decades. The United States and the Soviet Union fought together as allies in World War II, but just a few years after the war the two superpowers were aiming nuclear weapons at each other in a climate of mutual hostility and distrust. Fears of nuclear Armageddon led U.S. suburbanites to build backyard bomb shelters, while schoolteachers led young children in "duck and cover" drills, as if cowering under a wooden desk would prevent atomic annihilation. But the standoff with the Soviets also pushed both liberal and conservative politicians to tout consumer-driven free enterprise as "the essence of American freedom in the 1950s and a bulwark in the Cold War."[30] Conservative propaganda films of the period informed high school students that the logic of capitalist mass consumption was unassailable. If American teenagers developed "a clear understanding of our American system of capitalism," the narrator of *A Look at Capitalism* (1955) intoned, "then neither socialism nor communism ever will become established in America."[31] Americans learned to shudder at the thought of a totalitarian command economy, but even the most conservative politicians could not claim that Keynesian economics resembled Soviet communism. Furthermore, much of the government spending of the 1950s and 1960s was dedicated to military and defense projects supported by conservatives and liberals alike. A secret 1950 government document, NSC-68, laid out a blueprint for arming the United States to carry out an indefinite cold war against global communism, calling for massive defense spending to prepare for a constant state of war. Throughout the 1950s, defense spending accounted for one of every ten U.S. jobs, and anticommunism was an expected stance for both Republican and Democratic politicians.

For Nikita Khrushchev, Americans' anticommunist fears bordered on the absurd. State socialism, as Khrushchev saw it, had much in common with American capitalism in the 1950s. Both systems sought to provide the good life to their citizens through a combination of industrial productivity, worker incentives, and the logic of mass consumption driving ever-expanding economic growth. Indeed, in a 1957 interview Khrushchev informed a team of CBS television journalists that he greatly admired the productive capacity of American capitalism: "I like the very idea of our country now being able to compete with the United States, which is a very rich country indeed." But the American devotion to private property, its acceptance of inequality between the toiling masses and the owners of capitalist corporations, and its massive defense budgets were, according to Khrushchev, unacceptable means to the end of producing freedom from want. In the interview, Khrushchev went on to declare that his country's socialist approach to providing economic justice and security and upward mobility would eventually surpass the capitalist model, particularly if the United States accepted his notion of "peaceful coexistence" and allowed the Soviet Union to invest its resources in building up its farms and factories rather than producing intercontinental ballistic missiles and nuclear warheads. "Your grandsons will live under socialism in America, too. I can foretell this. Do not worry for your grandsons," Khrushchev chided. "They will only marvel at their grandfathers who did not understand such progressive teaching as the teaching of scientific socialism."[32]

Both the United States and the Soviet Union emerged from World War II convinced of the superiority of their approaches to providing their citizens with plenty. Americans chose a model premised on government oversight of a mass-consumption economy anchored by organized labor and big corporations. The Soviets under Khrushchev's rule chose a state-centered economic model that sought to provide for the material needs of worker-citizens. In contrast to the American system, Soviet leaders accepted the ideological tenets of communist thinking that prioritized public investment over private ownership, state control of industrial production, and collective enterprise. Like the Americans, though, Soviet leaders worshipped at the altar of consumer abundance (see Documents 7, 8, 13–15, 17, and 23).

THE CULTURE OF CONTAINMENT

In her memoir of growing up in the 1950s, Susan J. Douglas pinpointed the contradictory messages directed to young American girls. "I was told I was a member of a new, privileged generation," she wrote. "But at the same time, I was told that I really couldn't expect much more than to end up like my mother." In elementary school when the Soviet Union launched *Sputnik* in 1957, Douglas remembered how all children were expected to perform well in class: "As we . . . heard how if we didn't shape up fast we'd all be living on borscht, sharing an apartment the size of a refrigerator carton with all our relatives, and genuflecting to Nikita Khrushchev, one thing was clear: no one said, 'Just boys—just you boys study hard.'" At the same time, no one suggested that American girls grow up to be engineers. Everyone knew that the Soviet Union had female engineers, even doctors; but everyone also believed that Russian women were just plain unattractive. "It was because all their women were dead ringers for Mr. Potato Head that we knew their society was, at its heart, joyless, regimented, and bankrupt," Douglas recalled. "No one was going to let that happen here. . . . But it might if they took over."[33]

Douglas's remarks illustrate well how the cold war intersected with even the most private details of American life. The Soviet Union was a competitor in the race to secure affluence and abundance; it was also a cultural foil. While Americans enjoyed heaping dinner plates and ample suburban living space, the thinking went, Russians endured privation, crowded apartments, and authoritarian rule. While American women found joy in expressing their feminine charms and fulfilling their roles as mothers and housewives, Russian women submitted to state demands for workforce participation and thereby lost their female allure and sex appeal. The geopolitical stakes of the cold war might have originated in a divided Europe and a contested Asia, but as it evolved into a contest over living standards, the cold war also shaped the American home and the personal identities of its family members.

The era's overwhelmingly domestic ideology, and its celebration of conventional gender roles, was not a simple resumption of traditional patterns. Rather than returning to pre-Depression norms, the generation of young American couples who produced the famous "baby boom" between the 1940s and the early 1960s turned to marriage and child rearing with greater fervor than their parents, grandparents, or European counterparts. Indeed, the men and women who came of age during and just after World War II "were the most marrying generation on record."[34] Not only did these couples rush with unprecedented haste into domestic and conjugal commitment, they did so with striking conformity. Most were married by their mid-twenties and promptly had two to four children spaced closely together. The largest increase in the postwar birthrate, in fact, occurred among the most highly educated women; by 1956, one-quarter of white college women married while still in college. While general surveys of full-time homemakers revealed that they had no desire to trade their role for that of wage worker, surveys of educated women similarly indicated that they expected marriage and child rearing to offer avenues for creativity, managerial independence, and sexual fulfillment.

Television programs from the postwar era such as *Father Knows Best*, *Leave It to Beaver*, and *The Adventures of Ozzie and Harriet* have perpetuated images of stable and secure middle-class families in the 1950s, remarkably isolated from serious social conflict or psychological distress. But only by understanding the postwar years as an era of profound anxiety can we make sense of the novelty and tenacity of its domestic ideology. Marriage and babies, in short, offered security and reassurance in a world still haunted by a genocidal world war and now faced with the real threat of nuclear annihilation. The family also served as a social bulwark against communism and domestic subversion. Dangerous forces—unrestrained sexuality, unmanly and unwomanly behavior, political nonconformity—could be "contained" and neutralized through a traditional home, even as its individual members fully embraced the liberating possibilities of consumer abundance and family togetherness.

The culture of domestic containment also took shape as a reaction to the unprecedented visibility of women's wage work during World War II. Prewar women workers were predominantly single. If black or Hispanic, they were most likely to be domestic servants; if white, they worked in only a few employment categories such as teaching or nursing. As wartime mobilization revved up the economy and the military draft left it short of male labor, government and industry encouraged women to leave their homes for new occupations. Government propagandists devised icons such as Rosie the Riveter to urge women to patriotic duty on the factory lines. Riveting was a skilled job for which few employers were willing to train women, so Rosie did not represent the real work experiences of the many women who entered factory and service jobs during the war. Yet Rosie's plucky attitude and can-do spirit nonetheless sanctioned an experimental dose of "home front" womanhood decoupled from the actual home. The size of the female labor force more than doubled during the war years, and married women made up almost a majority of working women by its end.

These economic changes challenged prevailing gender ideology, sparking great cultural unease. Many commentators worried about the availability of jobs for returning servicemen, and others envisioned women as healers who should ultimately be available to assist the veterans' readjustment. "The men came home beat up," remembered one female New Yorker who looked unsuccessfully for a welding job after the war. "We were no longer comrades in arms; we were competitors for what little there was. . . . Being a woman, it was over for us."[35] Yet other women voluntarily left the workforce, many citing family responsibilities as their primary motive.[36] There existed a widespread understanding that women's work outside the home was never as valuable as their work within it. Many women probably agreed with the stridently anticommunist director of the FBI, J. Edgar Hoover, when he declared that mothers did "not need to put on overalls to prove [their] patriotism. . . . There should be a hot meal ready to serve and a mother fully dressed and ready to receive not only her own children but their friends."[37]

Hospitality and home cooking: these were indeed the quintessential products of feminine charm and motherly love. Did women feel obligated to perform these traditional duties, or did they make individual choices to work in primarily domestic settings? There is ample evidence to support the view that women welcomed homemaking and staked their identity as spouses, parents, and hosts on the products of their kitchens (see Documents 26 and 28–31). As much as the war opened up new employment opportunities, it barely affected the relationship of most middle-class women with their stoves. The well-stocked pantry and the private kitchen not only symbolized the abundance available in the United States; it also represented a widely shared understanding of female emancipation. Unlike Russian women, American women were not coerced into working outside the home, nor were they drafted into heavy labor or military service. They did not have to submit to communal cooking arrangements or to semi-raw foods hastily prepared after a day at the factory or in the field. They even had time to bake and to prepare desserts. Indeed, many American women resented the wartime allocation of scarce sugar stocks to commercial food producers, wishing instead to fill cake pans and jelly jars with their own handiwork.[38] Perhaps the noted food writer M. F. K. Fisher best captured the siren appeal of the cozy home kitchen when she declared that the returning serviceman "should know the sweet comforts of the flesh" and that his wife "must be lost in a sensual realization of all the magic she can evoke at table." A wife, Fisher continued, must "have the belief about her that preparing food, together or alone, is an act of dignity. . . . By the time women have felt their own power in their own kingdoms, they will know that they have never been slaves."[39]

There is also ample evidence to indicate that many women deeply resented the constriction of their opportunities outside the home after 1945. The majority of women who took up unconventional jobs during the war, after all, were not middle-class housewives; they were mainly working-class women who moved from lower-income occupations like waitressing and domestic service into higher-paid "men's" positions for the first time. Unlike their middle-class counterparts, these women did not have the option of leaving the workforce for the domestic sphere; at war's end, they found themselves relegated to what one historian has termed the "blue- and pink-collar ghetto of women's work."[40] A single or "family" wage large enough to support a full-time housewife was more of an aspiration than a reality for these families (see Document 27). Working-class women, in fact, constructed a significant new strand of feminism in the 1940s and 1950s, demanding fuller acceptance of women's work outside the home, more child-care options, and wages high enough for women alone to support their families.[41] But all women, even working ones, continued to shoulder the primary responsibility for housework and food preparation. One African American woman who resigned herself to a low-paying job after the war recalled how magazines "started telling you how to cook things that took a long time. . . . During the war they was [sic] telling you how you could cook dishes quickly and get on to work—now they were telling you how to cook dishes that took a *full day*."[42]

World War II in fact marked a permanent shift in women's labor force participation. Rates of female employment actually bounced back to wartime levels by the 1950s.[43] And despite the era's prevailing ideology of middle-class domesticity, this shift would not have occurred without the participation of many middle-class wives and mothers. Rising consumer expectations meant that more and more middle-class families combined the incomes of a male "breadwinner" and a female "cakewinner."[44] Ironically, women's wages supported the consumer prosperity of the postwar years even as the culture at large reveled in traditional gender roles. In fact, as mostly part-time workers, married women became a fluid and exploitable source of labor whose poor pay and lack of advancement could be justified by invoking their primary responsibilities as wives and mothers and their preference for flexible work hours. Within the family, women often took steps to disguise their economic contributions and to assure spouses that they were simply "helping out."[45] But women were in fact doing far more than "helping out." In 1950, married women accounted for just 36 percent of the female labor force; by 1960 this figure jumped to 52 percent.

Historians wrestle with the glaring contradiction between the culture of domesticity and the reality of women's rising labor force participation. The influential writer Betty Friedan, in her best-selling 1963 book, *The Feminine Mystique*, argued that postwar mass media, particularly women's magazines, left no ideological room for even highly educated women to consider careers outside the home.[46] Indeed, women's magazines routinely ran titles like "You Can't Have a Career and Be a Good Wife." For women considering a stint at work, one article put the choice bluntly: "Can you cook and wash dishes and sort laundry and be reasonably entertaining after the proverbial hard day at the office?"[47] Yet women's magazines also ran stories about female accomplishments in politics and in other public roles, suggesting that feminine fulfillment took a variety of legitimate forms.

Thus women heard contradictory messages during the 1950s. Some women certainly experienced the opportunity to choose public and professional identities, but the cold war nevertheless shaped an overarching consensus about the strategic importance of women's devotion to home and family. In 1960, for example, Under Secretary of Labor James T. O'Connell compared gender roles in the United States and the Soviet Union and noted that Soviet women accounted for 53 percent of that nation's workforce, with much higher representation in education and health-care professions. But rather than "applaud the USSR," O'Connell insisted that "much that supposedly separates us from the Communist world" would be lost if "a woman comes to be viewed first as a source of manpower, second as a mother." Echoing widespread American sentiments, he declared: "The highest calling of a woman's sex is in the home."[48]

The culture of domestic containment also took shape within a distinct material setting: the suburban home. While suburbanization was not a new phenomenon, the United States experienced an enormous upsurge in suburban growth in the postwar years. In 1940, only 13 percent of the U.S. population lived in the suburbs; by 1970, that figure had increased to 37 percent.[49] Though private developers exercised almost exclusive control over the construction and design of all those single-family homes, the federal government subsidized mortgages, covered much of the cost of new infrastructure such as roads and interstate highways, and sanctioned both the financial practices and the restrictive covenants that effectively barred people of color. By offering production advances to large-scale developers, the federal government also closed off alternative housing models, such as higher-density developments and planned towns, all of which were derided—in the words of Senator Joseph McCarthy—as too "communist."[50]

Though new suburbanites were not the majority in terms of numbers, they took cultural center stage as the postwar embodiment of the American dream and its emblematic consumer market. The suburban environment, in fact, fostered the widespread belief in "classlessness," which really meant that middle-class status no longer depended on one's occupation, but on one's lifestyle and possessions. And central to the iconic middle-class lifestyle was the female homemaker contentedly managing the household from her well-provisioned, color-coordinated, and appliance-laden kitchen (see Documents 26 and 28–31). By one estimate, Americans in the 1950s owned three-quarters of all the appliances and gadgets produced in the world.[51] And postwar home builders well understood that the kitchen, the primary destination for these purchases, would no longer be relegated to the back; it could now share the front of the house with the living room.[52]

The standard expectations for middle-class housekeeping, which included clean surfaces, freshly laundered clothing, and balanced meals, had originally evolved alongside the widespread practice of hiring outside help.[53] But it had long been a dream to "free" aspiring housewives of more limited means with labor-saving technology, especially electric appliances. As the supply of domestic servants declined over the first half of the twentieth century, and even more rapidly during World War II, women were inundated with messages about how a host of new "mechanical servants" had finally freed their creative energies for home-*making* rather than house*keeping*. In reality, the existence of all these electric appliances only raised the standards by which the homemaker was judged—by others and by herself (see Document 32).

The complex dance between labor-saving techniques and ever-higher standards of homemaking was certainly on display when it came to cooking in the 1950s. The vastly increased supply of packaged and semiprepared foods, for example, might have kept recipes simple and meals straightforward (see Document 31). "More servants are available to help with the work in U.S. kitchens than ever before," effused *Life* magazine in 1955. "They are the servants who come built into the frozen, canned, dehydrated, and pre-cooked food which lend busy women a thousand extra hands."[54] Women's magazines also reminded their readers to wean themselves from their mothers' cooking. "Nowadays a woman can get a whole meal on the table without knowing how to boil water," declared *Redbook*, "and the result will be perfectly adequate."[55] But even as sales of processed foods increased, they were not adopted as enthusiastically as producers and advertisers had expected. Many home cooks, it appeared, still valued the tastes and textures of "scratch" cooking, using convenience products only selectively (see Documents 30 and 32).[56] When packaged foods did appear in undisguised form, they often arrived as an incongruous mélange of sweet and savory ingredients assembled into elaborately structured dishes, such as the era's signature Jell-O molds, which advertised a wife's creativity and modernity.

Like their American counterparts, Soviet women after World War II were also called on to be devoted parents and flawless housekeepers.[57] The Khrushchev era, in fact, witnessed a momentous shift in Soviet ideology: contrary to earlier assumptions about the family withering away as socialism replaced capitalism, Soviet officials now asserted that the private home and traditional family could be a vehicle for proper socialist education.[58] Still, to a far greater degree than American women, Soviet women worked for wages outside the home. So many Soviet men were lost during the war that by its end in 1945 women constituted 57 percent of the USSR's total population and a majority of the total Soviet workforce. Between 1941 and 1950, 92 percent of all new workers were women.

Soviet women belonged to a society that in theory had liberated them: Communist revolutionary ideology held that the socialization of housework—that is, the entrusting of household tasks to paid workers—would emancipate women by allowing them to earn wages on equal terms with men (see Document 33). But although Soviet policymakers relied on women workers in industry and agriculture to pull the country through the war and its aftermath, the government never prioritized the public services that would have eased household burdens, even though Khrushchev-era officials validated women's participation in the workforce and promised an expansion of the services that would have allowed for their increasing visibility in Soviet public life. Women's wages, for example, were often set so low that only elite women had the wherewithal to participate fully in the revival of traditional femininity that took hold in the 1950s. Additionally, because officials never asked men to assume household or child-care duties, Soviet women usually worked more hours at home than they did on the job, many leaving their children alone or with a grandparent when they went to work because the state provided child-care facilities for only a fraction of those who required it. On a far larger scale than in the United States, where postwar prosperity never eradicated poverty and deprivation, Soviet women struggled daily with inadequate housing and paltry supplies of food and consumer items (see Document 22). Even though Khrushchev-era policy directed more funds to the building of single-family apartments, their cheap construction and shabby design quickly earned them the name *khrushchoby*, a blend of "Khrushchev" and the Russian word for "slum."[59]

Looming as an oasis of consumer bliss and homemaking fantasy just outside Moscow in 1959, the American Exhibition was indeed "dangerous stuff," in the words of one historian.[60] Soviet women who visited the American kitchens at Sokolniki Park may have agreed with Nikita Khrushchev when he ridiculed Richard Nixon's claim that Americans sought "to make easier the life of our housewives" (see Documents 14, 24, and 25). Yet there is also evidence that many Soviet women would very much have enjoyed an easier household life. Certainly, they looked forward to the future abundance that Khrushchev promised, and they took great pride in their country's advances in science and technology—achievements that they hoped were only temporarily paid for by the undersupply of public services and consumer goods (see Documents 33–36).

THE POLITICS OF FOOD AND FARMS

The kitchens on display in Moscow in July 1959 drew attention to the politics of abundance and to gender roles, but above all they demonstrated the importance of food to both American and Soviet economic planning. The United States emerged from World War II not only with the world's most productive industrial economy, but also with an unprecedented capacity to produce food and fiber. Postwar American agricultural productivity was crucial for supplying the abundance on display in supermarkets and kitchens in the 1950s, but it was also the subject of intense debates over the government's role in farm economies. The Soviet Union, meanwhile, emerged from World War II utterly devastated by the brutal land war against Germany, with both its industrial and agricultural base wiped out. By the late 1950s, the Soviet people had rebuilt their industrial might, and Nikita Khrushchev set his sights on using socialist measures to outpace American farmers. The race to agricultural supremacy for both countries entailed enormous transformations of domestic rural landscapes and livelihoods. It also pitted the two superpowers in a battle to demonstrate to the world's citizens that their respective economic models could feed a hungry world.

Postwar increases in American agricultural productivity and farm output were dramatic. The annual agricultural growth rate almost tripled in the decade after 1940, after holding steady at 1 percent the preceding sixty years. Even more astonishingly, this growth rate continued for the rest of the twentieth century—a record unmatched by any other economic sector.[61] Yields shot up all around: more crops per acre, more milk per cow, and more meat and eggs per pound of feed. So striking and sustained were these developments that one historian has labeled the postwar agricultural revolution the most important industrial revolution in all of American history.[62]

New technology powered the "revolution down on the farm." Advances in crop and animal breeding, increased use of chemical inputs such as fertilizers and pesticides, and more thorough mechanization contributed to skyrocketing levels of farm output. Commentators especially remarked on the factory-style production of red meat and poultry, everyday menu items whose availability and affordability were deeply symbolic of the nation's postwar affluence.[63] "Farmers are taking the big step from mechanization to automation in the raising of animals and fowl," *Time* magazine reported in 1959. Using "assembly-line techniques," farmers used "antibiotics, hormones, climate control, nutrition and plant and animal genetics" to produce meat and milk in quantities "that once nobody believed possible."[64]

Parallel revolutions in food processing and distribution also contributed to the low-price food economy. Between 1948 and 1958, grocery store sales rose more quickly than either population growth or increases in per capita income. Long-haul truckers whisked packaged meat, milk, and frozen orange juice directly to supermarkets, where consumers expected low prices and a wide variety of food products as a matter of course.[65] The supermarket, in the words of one early analyst, was a uniquely "American invention" that combined a departmentalized retail setting with self-service and a high sales volume.[66] Supermarkets quickly multiplied across the suburban landscape. By the mid-1960s, they accounted for almost three-fourths of all retail food sales, as mom-and-pop grocery stores disappeared from the street corners of cities and small towns. While the supermarket quickly became a common touchstone for critics of the era's plastic-wrapped abundance, it was nonetheless central to the postwar political economy of mass consumption (see Documents 18 and 19).

Few suburban consumers, however, understood the new political problems created by their nation's agricultural plenty. Agricultural incomes had historically lagged far behind the incomes of other workers, and since the Great Depression of the 1930s the federal government oversaw a complex system of commodity price supports intended to guarantee farmers a minimum return on their crops. While price supports and direct cash assistance had improved many farmers' economic position, an enormous flaw remained in the program: All participating farmers, no matter how large their operations, received these subsidies. Given the postwar technological revolution in agriculture, one acre now yielded two or even three times as much as in 1930. The results were predictable. Public policy encouraged a massive grain surplus for the federal government to manage.[67]

For agribusinesses involved in food processing and distribution, the "surplus problem" was obvious and the solution straightforward: The government should gradually remove itself from the business of setting farm prices and instead allow the market to regulate demand and supply. Others pointed out that only the biggest farm operations would benefit from those arrangements, because only high-volume producers could prosper in the low-price environment that would result from the removal of all supports. Indeed, the technological revolution in agriculture, mechanization especially, encouraged farmers to enlarge their operations and buy out their neighbors; smaller units were simply at a competitive disadvantage. Herein lay the crux of what many liberals and farm advocates called the "problem of plenty": Because owner-operated family farms sold only a limited amount of product, they required government assistance to remain viable. Should public policy intervene more aggressively to save family farms? Opinion was divided (see Documents 39 and 40). The issue was also complicated by cold war rhetoric. For many Americans, the family farm symbolized the essence of American democracy. "Nowhere," Democratic Senator William Proxmire proclaimed, "is this country's economic superiority to the Soviet Union more pronounced than in the great productivity of our electrified, power-driven, privately-owned family farm."[68] Such rhetoric concealed the uncomfortable fact that Americans valued both the abundance that technology and mechanization brought forth, as well as the family farms that these forces undermined.

While Americans debated how to dispose of "surplus" farm products in the 1950s and 1960s, Soviet leaders wrestled with the challenge of matching U.S. agricultural productivity. Khrushchev was determined to boost food production in his country without resorting to the brutal force of his predecessor, Joseph Stalin. Along with most Soviet citizens, Khrushchev remembered all too well the devastating famine of the 1930s that attended Stalin's farm collectivization campaigns, when millions of peasants were forced or cajoled to give up traditional forms of food production and work on scientifically managed, collectively owned farms. Low yields from the collective farms led to staggering losses of human and livestock lives, while another harrowing famine in 1946–1947 prompted Soviet officials to search long and hard for ways to improve farm output.[69] Among Khrushchev's boldest attempts to reframe farm policy after Stalin's death in 1953 was the Virgin Lands Campaign. Khrushchev ordered Soviet settlers to plow up tens of millions of acres of arid, largely uncultivated steppe lands in Kazakhstan, the Caucasus, and western Siberia and convert them to grain production. Alongside such dramatic actions, Khrushchev and his agricultural advisers continually tinkered with the structure of Soviet farming, providing farmers with economic incentives and machinery to boost yields. Although private land ownership was strictly off the table, Soviet agricultural reformers looked to American farming methods for inspiration, especially those practiced in the vast cornfields of Iowa (see Documents 37 and 38).[70]

The appeal of corn for the Soviets was not its suitability for feeding Soviet citizens directly, but as a source for fattening hogs and cattle. The meat and milk produced by these animals were the Kremlin's top priorities in the 1950s, as Soviets accustomed to years of subsistence on root vegetables and thin stews clamored for roasts, sausages, sour cream, and other high-status, high-protein foods. Especially after 1955, the meatier Soviet diet was to result from corn production. Over time, corn's intense thirst for nitrogen led to infertile fields and disastrously low crop yields. But from 1954 to 1958, favorable weather conditions and the audacious plow-up of the Virgin Lands Campaign helped boost Soviet grain production to impressive heights.[71]

Such successes gave Khrushchev the confidence in early 1957 to declare that, by the turn of the decade, the USSR would surpass the United States in per capita production of meat and milk. This ambitious goal spurred Soviet bureaucrats and collective farm managers to systematically inflate agricultural statistics to please state officials. But even as the nation announced to the world its alleged triumphs in agricultural productivity, Soviet food buyers continued to wait in long lines at state-run stores for foodstuffs that were often in dire shortage.

Khrushchev had bitten off more than he could chew. In 1960 and 1961, the Soviet Union witnessed its worst farm yields since the death of Stalin in 1953. State-run stores carried little or no meat and dairy products. Discontented citizens began to ridicule Khrushchev's repeated promises of plentiful food. Workers in Siberia hung posters on factory walls calling Khrushchev a "blabbermouth" and demanding immediate delivery of "that abundance you promised." In June 1962, Moscow central planners tried to encourage farmers to deliver more goods by raising food prices. Urban workers perceived the drastic rise in food costs as a betrayal. Widespread protests resulted. Workers walked out of factories, chanting "Meat! Meat! Raise our pay!"[72] A particularly violent episode took place in the factory city of Novocherkassk, where protesters suggested the people "use Khrushchev for sausage meat!" Red Army soldiers silenced the Novocherkassk protesters with machine-gun fire, killing twenty-two and wounding many more.[73] In 1963, Soviet leaders were humiliated when they had to ask U.S. officials to allow them to buy American grain (see Documents 41 and 42). Combined with his perceived weakness during the 1962 Cuban Missile Crisis and his failure to strengthen diplomatic ties with communist China, Khrushchev's inability to quell domestic economic unrest undermined his power at the Kremlin. By October 1964, Khrushchev was utterly discredited. He was unceremoniously removed from office by rival Leonid Brezhnev and sent to live out the rest of his days in retirement, ignored by the new regime (see Document 43).[74]

Soviet officials worked hard to dismiss the legacy of Nikita Khrushchev after his ouster from the Kremlin. But in the summer of 1959, when Khrushchev shared the world stage with Richard Nixon at Sokolniki Park, his boasts of imminent socialist consumer abundance could not be ignored. From today's post–cold war perspective, the thought of two world leaders debating the merits of communism versus capitalism in a canary-yellow kitchen may seem somewhat surreal. When Khrushchev and Nixon faced off at the Kitchen Debate in July 1959, however, both understood just how real the stakes of the economic cold war were.

NOTES

[1] "Nixon Arrival Statement," July 23, 1959, Folder 3, Box 1, RG 306 Entry 54, National Archives II, College Park, Md.

[2] Stephen J. Whitfield, *The Culture of the Cold War*, 2nd ed. (Baltimore: Johns Hopkins University Press, 1996), 72.

[3] "The U.S. in Moscow: Russia Comes to the Fair," *Time*, August 3, 1959, 14; Cristina Carbone, "Staging the Kitchen Debate: How Splitnik Got Normalized in the United States," in *Cold War Kitchen: Americanization, Technology, and European Users*, ed. Ruth Oldenziel and Karin Zachmann (Cambridge, Mass.: MIT Press, 2009), 70.

[4] In this text we use *communist* to refer to the Marxist-Leninist political ideology followed by the Soviet Union from 1922 to 1991, in which a centralized one-party state controlled the means of production in order to serve the needs of the working class. The Soviet Union had a *socialist* economy, meaning that its economic activities were owned and managed in common, rather than privately. Socialism could and does take many forms, however, ranging from cooperative ownership to full state control of enterprise, without necessarily relying on communist ideology or political structures.

[5] John L. Gaddis, *We Now Know: Rethinking Cold War History* (New York: Oxford University Press, 1997).

[6] Melvyn P. Leffler, *For the Soul of Mankind: The United States, the Soviet Union, and the Cold War* (New York: Hill and Wang, 2007).

[7] George F. Kennan ("X"), "The Sources of Soviet Conduct," *Foreign Affairs* 25 (July 1947): 580–81.

[8] Walter LaFeber, *The Origins of the Cold War, 1941–1947: A Historical Problem with Interpretation and Documents* (New York: John Wiley, 1971), 155.

[9] Michael J. Hogan, *A Cross of Iron: Harry S. Truman and the Origins of the National Security State, 1945–1954* (Cambridge, U.K.: Cambridge University Press, 1998); Walter LaFeber, *America, Russia, and the Cold War, 1945–2006* (New York: McGraw-Hill, 2008).

[10] Tony Judt, *Postwar: A History of Europe Since 1945* (New York: Penguin, 2005).

[11] Kenneth Osgood, *Total Cold War: Eisenhower's Secret Propaganda Battle at Home and Abroad* (Lawrence: University Press of Kansas, 2006), 61.

[12] Walter L. Hixson, *Parting the Curtain: Propaganda, Culture, and the Cold War, 1945–1961* (New York: St. Martin's Press, 1997); Greg Castillo, *Cold War on the Home Front: The Soft Power of Midcentury Design* (Minneapolis: University of Minnesota Press, 2010); Laura A. Belmonte, *Selling the American Way: U.S. Propaganda and the Cold War* (Philadelphia: University of Pennsylvania Press, 2008).

[13] U.S. Department of State, *Foreign Relations of the United States, 1946* (Washington, D.C., 1969), 701–3.

[14] Ellen Schrecker, *The Age of McCarthyism: A Brief History with Documents* (New York: Bedford/St. Martin's, 2002).

[15] Kathyrn S. Olmsted, *Real Enemies: Conspiracy Theories and American Democracy, World War I to 9/11* (New York: Oxford University Press, 2011).

[16] Rick Perlstein, *Nixonland: The Rise of a President and the Fracturing of America* (New York: Scribner, 2008), 28, 34–35.

[17] William Taubman, *Khrushchev: The Man and His Era* (New York: W. W. Norton, 2003), 45–235.

[18] Ibid., 427.

[19] Susan E. Reid, "The Khrushchev Kitchen: Domesticating the Scientific-Technological Revolution," *Journal of Contemporary History* 40 (April 2005): 289.

[20] Nikita Khrushchev, Speech to the Plenary Session of the Central Committee of the Soviet Communist Party, *Pravda*, September 15, 1953, 1–6. Translated in *Current Digest of the Soviet Press* 5, no. 39: 11.

[21] Taubman, *Khrushchev*, 262.

[22] Hixson, *Parting the Curtain*, 179. A video of Khrushchev's teasing of Nixon can be found at www.c-spanvideo.org/program/110721-1 (03:24).

[23] Nikita Khrushchev, "To Overtake and Outstrip in the Next Years the United States of America in the Per Capita Output of Meat, Butter, and Milk," Leningrad, May 22, 1957, Foreign Broadcast Information Service, *Daily Report, Foreign Radio Broadcasts*, May 24, 1957, pp. CC5, 7, 8, 11.

[24] Elizabeth Borgwardt, *A New Deal for the World: America's Vision for Human Rights* (Cambridge, Mass.: Harvard University Press, 2005), 46–53; Franklin D. Roosevelt: "Address to the International Labor Organization," November 6, 1941, American Presidency Project, www.presidency.ucsb.edu/ws/?pid=16037.

[25] Roland Marchand, "Visions of Classlessness, Quests for Dominion: American Popular Culture, 1945–1960," in *Reshaping America: Society and Institutions, 1945–1960,*

ed. Robert H. Bremner and Gary W. Reichard (Columbus: Ohio State University Press, 1982), 163–90.

[26] Lizabeth Cohen, *A Consumers' Republic: The Politics of Mass Consumption in Post-war America* (New York: Knopf, 2003).

[27] Perlstein, *Nixonland*, 28.

[28] Meg Jacobs, *Pocketbook Politics: Economic Citizenship in Twentieth-Century America* (Princeton, N.J.: Princeton University Press, 2005).

[29] Ira Katznelson, *When Affirmative Action Was White: An Untold History of Racial Inequality in Twentieth-Century America* (New York: W. W. Norton, 2005).

[30] Lawrence B. Glickman, *Buying Power: A History of Consumer Activism in America* (Chicago: University of Chicago Press, 2009), 264.

[31] *A Look at Capitalism*, produced by National Education Program, film, 1955. Available at www.archive.org/details/LookatCa1955.

[32] Nikita Khrushchev, June 3, 1957, interview on CBS television, Foreign Broadcast Information Service, *Daily Report, Foreign Radio Broadcasts*, June 4, 1957, pp. BB4, 7.

[33] Susan J. Douglas, *Where the Girls Are: Growing Up Female with the Mass Media* (New York: Random House, 1994), 25, 22.

[34] Elaine Tyler May, *Homeward Bound: American Families in the Cold War Era* (New York: Basic Books, 1988), 20.

[35] *The Life and Times of Rosie the Riveter*, produced and directed by Connie Field, Clarity Films, 1980.

[36] David M. Kennedy, *Freedom from Fear: The American People in Depression and War, 1929–1945* (New York: Oxford University Press, 1999), 780.

[37] J. Edgar Hoover, "Mothers . . . Our Only Hope," *Women's Home Companion*, January 1944, reprinted in Nancy A. Walker, *Women's Magazines, 1940–1960: Gender Roles and the Popular Press* (New York: Bedford/St. Martin's, 1998), 46.

[38] Amy Bentley, *Eating for Victory: Food Rationing and the Politics of Domesticity* (Urbana: University of Illinois Press, 1998).

[39] M. F. K. Fisher, "The Lively Art of Eating," *Harper's Bazaar*, November 1944, reprinted in Walker, *Women's Magazines*, 159, 160.

[40] Dorothy Sue Cobble, *The Other Women's Movement: Workplace Justice and Social Rights in Modern America* (Princeton, N.J.: Princeton University Press, 2004), 13.

[41] Ibid.

[42] *The Life and Times of Rosie the Riveter*.

[43] Susan M. Hartmann, "Women's Employment and the Domestic Ideal in the Early Cold War Years," in Joanne Meyerowitz, ed., *Not June Cleaver: Women and Gender in Postwar America, 1945–1960* (Philadelphia: Temple University Press, 1994), 86.

[44] Judith Sealander, *As Minority Becomes Majority: Federal Reaction to the Phenomenon of Women in the Work Force, 1920–1963* (Westport, Conn.: Greenwood Press, 1983), 133.

[45] Ruth Rosen, *The World Split Open: How the Modern Women's Movement Changed America* (New York: Penguin, 2000), 21.

[46] Betty Friedan, *The Feminine Mystique* (New York: Norton, 1963). Also see Stephanie Coontz, *A Strange Stirring:* The Feminine Mystique *and American Women at the Dawn of the 1960s* (New York: Basic Books, 2011).

[47] "You Can't Have a Career and Be a Good Wife," *Ladies' Home Journal*, January 1944, reprinted in Walker, *Women's Magazines*, 71; "The Married Woman Goes Back to Work," *Woman's Home Companion*, October 1956, reprinted in Walker, *Women's Magazines*, 95.

[48] James O'Connell, quoted in Sealander, *As Minority Becomes Majority*, 139–40.

[49] Becky M. Nicolaides and Andrew Wiese, *The Suburb Reader* (New York: Routledge, 2006), 2.

[50] Nicolaides and Wiese, *Suburb Reader*, 257.

[51] Dolores Hayden, "Building the American Way: Public Subsidy, Private Space" (2004), in Nicolaides and Wiese, *Suburb Reader*, 278.

52 Barbara M. Kelly, *Expanding the American Dream* (1993), in Nicolaides and Wiese, *Suburb Reader*, 286.

53 Phyllis Palmer, *Domesticity and Dirt: Housewives and Domestic Servants in the United States, 1920–1945* (Philadelphia: Temple University Press, 1989).

54 "Ways to Cut Down Kitchen Work," *Life*, January 3, 1955, 17.

55 Jane Whitbread and Vivian Cadden, "Granny's on the Pan," *Redbook*, November 1951, reprinted in Walker, *Women's Magazines*, 169.

56 Laura Shapiro, *Something from the Oven: Reinventing Dinner in 1950s America* (New York: Penguin, 2004).

57 Greta Bucher, *Women, the Bureaucracy, and Daily Life in Postwar Moscow, 1945–1953* (Boulder, Colo.: East European Monographs, distributed by Columbia University Press, 2006), 17.

58 Melanie Ilič, Susan E. Reid, and Lynne Attwood, eds., *Women in the Khrushchev Era* (New York: Palgrave Macmillan, 2004).

59 Lynne Attwood, *Gender and Housing in Soviet Russia: Private Life in a Public Space* (Manchester, U.K.: Manchester University Press, 2010), 155.

60 Barbara A. Engel, *Women in Russia, 1700–2000* (New York: Cambridge University Press, 2004), 241.

61 Bruce L. Gardner, *American Agriculture in the Twentieth Century: How It Flourished and What It Cost* (Cambridge, Mass.: Harvard University Press, 2002).

62 Paul Conkin, *A Revolution Down on the Farm: The Transformation of American Agriculture Since 1929* (Lexington: University Press of Kentucky, 2008), 97.

63 Data on per capita food availability since 1909 is available from the Economic Research Service, U.S. Department of Agriculture, Food Availability (Per Capita) Data System, www.ers.usda.gov/Data/FoodConsumption.

64 "Agriculture: The Pushbutton Cornucopia," *Time*, March 9, 1959, 74.

65 Shane Hamilton, *Trucking Country: The Road to America's Wal-Mart Economy* (Princeton, N.J.: Princeton University Press, 2008).

66 Rom J. Markin, *The Supermarket: An Analysis of Growth, Development, and Change* (Pullman: Washington State University Bureau of Economic and Business Research, 1968).

67 "Acquisition and Disposal by CCC of Surplus Farm Products," ASCS Background Information, BI No. 3, December 1961, Box 1182, George McGovern Papers, Mudd Library, Princeton, N.J.

68 Joint Economic Committee, *1961 Joint Economic Report*, 87th Cong., 1st sess., May 2, 1961, H. Rpt. 328.

69 Lazar Volin, *A Century of Russian Agriculture: From Alexander II to Khrushchev* (Cambridge, Mass.: Harvard University Press, 1970).

70 Stephen J. Frese, "Comrade Khrushchev and Farmer Garst: East-West Encounters Foster Agricultural Exchange," *History Teacher*, November 2004.

71 Lazar Volin, "Khrushchev and the Soviet Agricultural Scene," in *Soviet and East European Agriculture*, ed. Jerzy F. Karcz (Berkeley: University of California Press, 1967), 14–15.

72 Taubman, *Khrushchev*, 480–81, 507, 516, 519–20.

73 Reid, "Cold War in the Kitchen," 251.

74 Taubman, *Khrushchev*, 615–17.

PART TWO

The Documents

1

The Kitchen Debate

In 1958, a slight thaw in relations between the United States and the Soviet Union emerged when the two countries agreed to a program of cultural exchange, including plans to stage national exhibitions on each other's soil. In June 1959, the Soviet National Exhibition in New York City allowed Americans to see *Sputnik I* firsthand, a not-so-subtle reminder of the fear that had gripped the United States in October 1957 when the Soviets' successful launch of the first earth-orbiting satellite aroused concerns about American inferiority in scientific and technological development.

A month after the Soviet exhibition opened in New York, U.S. Vice President Richard Nixon traveled to Moscow to inaugurate the American National Exhibition in Sokolniki Park. Anchored by a futuristic geodesic dome designed by Buckminster Fuller, the American pavilion allowed millions of Soviet visitors to view a suburban ranch-style home, American-style kitchens, shiny appliances, color televisions, and a host of other consumer goods. Orchestrated by the U.S. Information Agency (USIA) in cooperation with private corporations, the exhibition was a central component of a broad propaganda campaign initiated under the Eisenhower administration to "win" the cold war through global promotion of the "American way of life."

As Nixon toured the displays of American abundance in Sokolniki Park, he and Soviet Premier Nikita Khrushchev alternated between friendly banter and bombastic declarations of the superiority of their countries' economic systems. The verbal sparring between Nixon and Khrushchev was quickly dubbed the "Kitchen Debate" by journalists, although the two leaders traded barbs in a live television studio and other locations as well as in the model kitchens. The kitchen was nonetheless central to the debate, as both Nixon and Khrushchev staked out consumer prosperity as a key battleground in the ideological contest between the two cold war superpowers.

Selling the American Way

1

LLEWELLYN E. THOMPSON

U.S. Ambassador's Telegram on Plans for the American National Exhibition

November 17, 1958

Serving as U.S. ambassador to Moscow from 1957 to 1962 (and again in the late 1960s), diplomat Llewellyn E. Thompson witnessed firsthand the cold war propaganda campaigns waged by the United States and the Soviet Union. In this telegram sent to the U.S. State Department and read by USIA officials, Thompson lays out his concerns regarding the planned American National Exhibition in Moscow.

Having examined the text of the basic policy guidance for the US exhibit in Moscow,[1] I wish to submit the following comments. It would be scarcely possible in my opinion to overstate the importance of this opportunity to hold a US exhibit in Moscow provided we succeed in presenting one that is appropriate. It can, I believe, have an explosive effect upon the Soviet public and lead to important political consequences of incalculable benefit to the US. The mere fact that such an exhibit is contemplated, which appears to be well known in Moscow, has aroused the

---

[1] This "basic policy guidance" document was a confidential USIA memorandum of January 1959 that detailed the "secret" primary objective of the American National Exhibition: to "contribute to existing pressures in the long run toward a reorientation of the Soviet system in the direction of greater freedom." The memo noted that this potentially undiplomatic objective was "for planning purposes and not for publication." The public was to be told that the objective was "to increase understanding by the peoples of the Soviet Union of the American people . . . and the broad scope of American life. "

From Llewellyn E. Thompson to Department of State, November 17, 1958, Folder 2, Box 2, RG 306 Entry 54, National Archives II, College Park, Md.

most intense interest on the part of all of our Soviet contacts including the top levels of the Soviet Government and the Communist Party.

I should like to submit the following comments on the basic policy guidance as well as some general comments on the basic plan. It would appear to me that in general there is too much emphasis upon the propaganda aspects of the exhibit and that an effort should be made to make our propaganda objectives less evident. I agree completely with the statement of the main objective but am inclined to question the primary theme of "freedom of choice and expression." This is admittedly a desirable point to bring out in the exhibit but I question that this is the primary means of achieving the objective stated. There is no possibility, short of revolution, for the Soviet people to achieve freedom of choice and expression and if carried out literally this theme would constitute a direct attack upon the Soviet system. In my opinion our primary theme should be that, regardless of how it is achieved, the US has superiority in both quality and quantity in all aspects of its cultural and economic life. We should endeavor to make the Soviet people dissatisfied with the share of the Russian pie which they now receive and make them realize that the slight improvements projected in their standard of living are only a drop in the bucket to what they could and should have. I do not of course see any objection to the freedom of choice theme being subtly and indirectly expressed. . . .

Throughout the plan there is strong emphasis on photographs of people. We should remember that the Soviets have used *ad nauseam* the technique of showing happy, smiling faces, and I suggest that less use be made of this technique than is apparently contemplated in the draft plan. Of course, wide use can be made of photographs showing the American scene which indirectly will put across many of the important points which we hope to achieve, such as the number of automobiles outside of factories and other more subtle points. . . .

Under heading 4, America Consumes, it is questioned whether the items about market approach, consumer research, advertising, etc., are appropriate or will have much interest for the Soviet audience. In item 3 under this heading it is not clear whether merely photographs of supermarkets are to be shown or whether there would be an attempt to actually set up a model supermarket. I believe that it would be highly useful to show a typical store specializing in one particular item such as kitchen utensils or hardware. I would doubt whether the logistic problem and expense would justify attempting actually to operate a supermarket as has been done elsewhere, although, if space permits the setting up of such a market, it might be useful, particularly in order to show the types of display equipment used. The Soviets are interested in vending machines, and it might be possible to consider using these in connection with the sale of souvenirs if this is decided upon.

2

OFFICE OF THE AMERICAN
NATIONAL EXHIBITION IN MOSCOW

Kitchens of Today and Tomorrow Slated for Moscow Exhibition

February 9, 1959

This press release, intended to attract media attention, explains why U.S. planners believed model kitchens would have a powerful impact on Soviet visitors to the American National Exhibition in Moscow.

Soviet women soon will get a chance to see that American scientific progress is not limited to a "man's world." Modern U.S. inventions, they'll observe, also are making life easier for the housewife.

The American National Exhibition in Moscow this summer will feature both a "kitchen of today" and a "kitchen of the future." They are the RCA Whirlpool Mrs. America All-Gas Kitchen and the RCA Whirlpool Miracle Kitchen—complete with such electronic advances as a "mechanical maid" and an "automatic meal maker."

Both kitchens will be seen for the first time in the USSR at Moscow's Sokolniki Park. An estimated 3 1/2 million persons will visit the six-week-long exhibition.

The RCA Whirlpool Miracle Kitchen is the "kitchen of the future" which drew crowds at the Milan Fair in Italy last year. It is a collection of electronic contrivances that operate by a push of a button or a wave of the hand.

From Office of the American National Exhibition in Moscow, press release, "Kitchens of Today and Tomorrow Slated for Moscow Exhibition," February 9, 1959, Folder 1, Box 1, RG 306 Entry 54, National Archives II, College Park, Md.

The Mrs. America Kitchen will give the Soviets a look at the kind of appliances that are in use in millions of American homes today. Demonstrators will give spectators a taste of "blini" [small savory pancakes] and other Russian specialties that are simple to prepare.

Demonstrators in both kitchens will speak Russian. The RCA Whirlpool Corporation also is providing a million copies of a Russian-language brochure describing both kitchens and containing typical American recipes.

3

OFFICE OF THE AMERICAN
NATIONAL EXHIBITION IN MOSCOW

Cooking Display in Moscow to Feature American Dishes
May 13, 1959

Under the Eisenhower administration's cold war propaganda campaigns, American corporations were regularly called on to contribute funds, staff, and products to USIA exhibits. This press release mentions several U.S. firms that used the American National Exhibition in Moscow as a forum for advertising how the "average American homemaker" used their products.

The aroma of fried chicken and freshly-baked pies will lead Soviet crowds to a busy kitchen at the American National Exhibition in Moscow this summer.

Through the combined efforts of General Mills, Inc., Minneapolis, Minnesota, and the General Foods Corporation, White Plains, New York, Soviet visitors will see for themselves how an American housewife can dish up a full-course dinner in a matter of minutes. What's more,

From Office of the American National Exhibition in Moscow, press release, "Cooking Display in Moscow to Feature American Dishes," May 13, 1959, Folder 1, Box 1, RG 306 Entry 54, National Archives II, College Park, Md.

they'll be invited to sample the cooking—110 varieties of food adding up to seven tons.

The continuous food preparation demonstrations will take place in the Whirlpool gas kitchen in the main exhibition hall. To fill the cupboards and freezers, General Foods Corporation is sending 10,000 pounds of frozen foods—beef pies, fish, turkey and chicken dinners, 32 different fruit and vegetable products, and many other specialties.

General Mills, Inc., is sending more than 4,500 packages of mixes for cakes, frostings, cookies, cereals—everything from biscuits to Boston Cream pie. With this shipment will go a large supply of cookbooks.

The food items, found in practically any American grocery store, will be prepared and cooked in front of Soviet spectators. According to present plans, those who are elsewhere on the exhibition grounds may be able to watch the cooking on RCA closed-circuit color television.

Chairwoman of the demonstrations will be Barbara Sampson, home economist for the Birds Eye division of General Foods, working in close association with Marylee Duehring, supervisor of product counselors of the Betty Crocker Kitchens, General Mills.

They will train a staff of six young women—five Soviet girls and one Russian-speaking American—as their assistants.

Wearing brightly-colored cotton dresses, the demonstrators will work in a specially designed yellow-and-white kitchen, featuring gas appliances and such homey touches as potted plants and starched curtains. They'll take turns at the kitchen stove from 11 a.m. to 10 p.m. daily for six weeks—showing an estimated 3 1/2 million persons the part that "convenience foods," the mixes and frozen products, play in the life of the average American homemaker and her family.

The American National Exhibition, which opens in Moscow's Sokolniki Park July 25, has numerous other exhibits and demonstrations designed to further Soviet understanding of life in America.

4

JERRY MARLATT

Letter to President Dwight Eisenhower

July 10, 1959

---

*American citizen Jerry Marlatt, typing on the stationery of the Flossmoor
(Illinois) Country Club, expressed his own ideas to President Eisenhower
about what should be on display at the American National Exhibition.
Many such suggestions arrived on officials' desks, but the key decisions
about what to include at the Moscow exhibit were made by USIA staff in
conversation with the corporate leaders who contributed funds and goods
to the project.*

Hon. Dwight David Eisenhower
President, The United States of America
The White House
1600 Pennsylvania Avenue
Washington, D.C.

Dear Mr. President:

I noted with concern the "hurrah" over the exhibits of the United States
at the Russian Trade Fair and then was astounded when I saw this weeks
[*sic*] edition of LOOK Magazine.

   I think that we are being utterly ridiculous in taking a $2 million dollar
kitchen, costly automobiles, paintings and other items to show to people
who we are trying to be friendly with. If I suddenly parked a Cadillac in
my driveway, my wife sported a new mink coat, and I displayed other
items of wealth I do not think my neighbors would be impressed, nor
would it create a friendly atmosphere or harmonious feeling of trying
to make a fair exchange of impressions. We cannot make friends by dis-
playing our wealth, and I think that it is really silly to take something like
this to be displayed to people we are trying to impress as being friendly,
cordial, and understanding.

From Jerry Marlatt to Dwight Eisenhower, July 10, 1959, Folder 9, Box 1, RG 306 Entry
54, National Archives II, College Park, Md.

Why don't you let a typical American family make up an exhibit, fly the family and their exhibit to the fair for one week, and I assure you that it will create more good will, be more talked about and better display the true examples of America and our democratic ideals than this $2 million kitchen.

I feel that I, and my family are fairly typical. Statistics: Married 13 years, 2 daughters, occupation: Club Manager, Salary $10,000 per year. WW 2 Vet, 25 year conventional mortgage and all of that stuff.

What would I take to show the Russians at a fair, or any Europeans? Listen to this list Mr. President:

1. Striped Tooth paste

2. Sugar Coated Cereal

3. Dividend Check from 10 shares of Greyhound Stock

4. My 12 foot mortgage payment book

5. My Stereo camera and slides

6. My tape recorder

7. A Dari-Queen cone

8. A 16 oz. U.S. Prime Sirloin Steak

9. Pink Lemonade (Frozen)

10. My G.I. insurance policy

11. A pre-packaged and frozen TV Dinner

12. A hi-fidelity record player and 24 records of asst. [assorted] jazz, American Folk Songs, Spirituals and music of the '40s

13. A copy of Playboy Magazine. (We have seen so many pictures of undraped European gals, let's show them some American girls in their more primitive state.)

14. A set of golf clubs, and a pull cart

15. My 1959 income tax return

16. Two plump daughters, ages 10 and 11 complete with hula hoops, Brownie and Girl Scout outfits, and a Monopoly set and polio shots.

17. A picture of my $13,500 house and my 1959 Ford Station Wagon

18. Pictures of the Statue of Liberty, Grand Canyon, Niagara Falls, The Chicago skyline, and a slum clearance project.

19. A copy of the wording at the base of the Statue of Liberty about "give us your tired, your humble masses, etc."

20. A United States Defense bond

All things Mr. President which are available to all of us here in this great country of ours. Let them see how average Americans live and not present 2 million dollar kitchens, fabulous automobiles, Walt Disney extravaganzas and controversial paintings. Don't send Louie Armstrong, jugglers, and Vice President Nixon or 10 governors, but send them typical, living, honest to goodness, truthful and democratic loving Americans.

Let me smile and tell a Russian that I make $10,000 per year, pay about $1200 income tax, and get Blue Cross Insurance for $10.10 per quarter and can write to the President, quit my job when ever I want, and boo the umpire at a ball game and let my two daughters talk to those Russian kids and give them a Dari-Queen and let them play with their Girl Scout compass and let that Russian woman let my wife show her how to make a $35.00 dress from a McCalls pattern for 39¢ and man I am sure those Russians will look at us and smile and say I know this man don't want war, or atom bombs or his pooch floating around in a Sputnik. . . .

Nixon Goes to Moscow

5

The Two Worlds: A Day-Long Debate
July 25, 1959

American journalists quickly gave the label "Kitchen Debate" to the verbal sparring between U.S. Vice President Richard Nixon and Soviet Premier Nikita Khrushchev at the opening of the American National Exhibition. Because most of their conversation was unscripted and only a portion of it was captured on television cameras, no completely authoritative transcription of their discussions exists. In this account, the New York Times *offered a relatively thorough rendering of Nixon's and Khrushchev's remarks by compiling reports from various journalists and news wire services.*

From "The Two Worlds: A Day-Long Debate," *New York Times*, July 25, 1959, 1, 3.

Mr. Nixon was welcomed at the Premier's office in the Kremlin in the morning. There the principals exchanged greetings and handshakes, Mr. Nixon saying a few words in Russian.

Khrushchev: "You have learned some Russian."

Nixon (indicating with slightly separated fingers): "Just this much."

Khrushchev: "This is our first meeting. I welcome you. We hope your visit will be helpful in improving relations."

More pleasantries followed, Mr. Khrushchev remarking, "I hear you have been to the market place." Then reporters and photographers were ushered out and the statesmen had a private talk.

A Trade of Gibes about Trade

On arriving at the gate of the American National Exhibition later in the morning, Mr. Khrushchev voiced a gibe about the United States ban on the shipment of strategic goods to the Soviet Union.

Khrushchev: "Americans have lost their ability to trade. Now you have grown older and you don't trade the way you used to. You need to be invigorated."

Nixon: "You need to have goods to trade." . . .

Khrushchev: "We want to live in peace and friendship with Americans because we are the two most powerful countries, and if we live in friendship then other countries will also live in friendship. But if there is a country that is too war-minded we could pull its ears a little and say: Don't you dare; fighting is not allowed now; this is a period of atomic armament; some foolish one could start a war and then even a wise one couldn't finish the war. Therefore, we are governed by this idea in our policy—internal and foreign. How long has America existed? Three hundred years?"

Nixon: "One hundred and fifty years."

They Will Wave as They Pass U.S.

Khrushchev: "One hundred and fifty years? Well, then, we will say America has been in existence for 150 years and this is the level she has reached. We have existed not quite forty-two years and in another seven years we will be on the same level as America.

"When we catch you up, in passing you by, we will wave to you. Then if you wish we can stop and say: Please follow up. Plainly speaking, if you want capitalism you can live that way. That is your own affair and doesn't concern us. We can still feel sorry for you but since you don't understand us—live as you do understand.

"We are all glad to be here at the exhibition with Vice President Nixon. I personally, and on behalf of my colleagues, express my thanks for the President's message. I have not as yet read it but I know before-hand that it contains good wishes. I think you will be satisfied with your visit and if—I cannot go on without saying it—if you would not take such a decision [proclamation by the United States Government of Captive Nations Week, a week of prayer for peoples enslaved by the Soviet Union][1] which has not been thought out thoroughly, as was approved by Congress, your trip would be excellent. But you have churned the water yourselves—why this was necessary God only knows.

"What happened? What black cat crossed your path and confused you? But that is your affair, we do not interfere with your problems. [Wrapping his arms about a Soviet workman] Does this man look like a slave laborer? [Waving at others] With men with such spirit how can we lose?"

Exchange of Ideas Urged by Nixon

Nixon (pointing to American workmen): "With men like that we are strong. But these men, Soviet and American, work together well for peace, even as they have worked together in building this exhibition. This is the way it should be.

"Your remarks are in the tradition of what we have come to expect—sweeping and extemporaneous. Later on we will both have an opportunity to speak and consequently I will not comment on the various points that you raised, except to say this—this color television is one of the most advanced developments in communication that we have.

"I can only say that if this competition in which you plan to out-strip us is to do the best for both of our peoples and for peoples everywhere, there must be a free exchange of ideas. After all, you don't know everything—"

Khrushchev: "If I don't know everything, you don't know anything about communism except fear of it."

Nixon: "There are some instances where you may be ahead of us, for example in the development of the thrust of your rockets for the

---

[1] Whether or not the 1959 congressional declaration of the third week of July as Captive Nations Week was intended to provoke Soviet ire just days before Nixon's visit to Moscow, it certainly did so by effectively calling for the overthrow of all the communist governments of Eastern Europe. Sometimes referred to as Enslaved Nations Week, the tradition begun under President Eisenhower was adopted by President Kennedy and has continued through every presidential administration to date.

investigation of outer space; there may be some instances in which we are ahead of you—in color television, for instance."

Khrushchev: "No, we are up with you on this, too. We have bested you in one technique and also in the other."

Nixon: "You see, you never concede anything."

Khruschchev: "I do not give up."

Appearances on TV Are Suggested

Nixon: "Wait till you see the picture. Let's have far more communication and exchange in this very area that we speak of. We should hear you more on our television. You should hear us more on yours."

Khrushchev: "That's a good idea. Let's do it like this. You appear before our people. We will appear before your people. People will see and appreciate this."

Nixon: "There is not a day in the United States when we cannot read what you say. When Kozlov[2] was speaking in California about peace, you were talking here in somewhat different terms. This was reported extensively in the American press. Never make a statement here if you don't want it to be read in the United States. I can promise you every word you say will be translated into English."

Khrushchev: "I doubt it. I want you to give your word that this speech of mine will be heard by the American people."

Nixon (shaking hands on it): "By the same token, everything I say will be translated and heard all over the Soviet Union?"

Khrushchev: "That's agreed."

Nixon: "You must not be afraid of ideas."

Khrushchev: "We are telling you not to be afraid of ideas. We have no reason to be afraid. We have already broken free from such a situation."

Nixon: "Well, then, let's have more exchange of them. We are all agreed on that. All right? All right?"

Khrushchev: "Fine. [Aside] Agree to what? All right, I am in agreement. But I want to stress what I am in agreement with. I know that I am dealing with a very good lawyer. I also want to uphold my own miner's flag so that the coal miners can say: Our man does not concede."

Nixon: "No question about that."

[2] Frol R. Kozlov, a protégé of Khrushchev and a high-ranking official in the Communist Party of the Soviet Union.

Khrushchev: "You are a lawyer for capitalism and I am a lawyer for communism. Let's compete."

Vice President Protests Filibuster

Nixon: "The way you dominate the conversation you would make a good lawyer yourself. If you were in the United States Senate you would be accused of filibustering."

Nixon (halting Khrushchev at model kitchen in model house): "You had a very nice house in your exhibition in New York. My wife and I saw and enjoyed it very much. I want to show you this kitchen. It is like those of our houses in California."

Khrushchev (after Nixon called attention to a built-in panel-controlled washing machine): "We have such things."

Nixon: "This is the newest model. This is the kind which is built in thousands of units for direct installation in the houses."

He added that Americans were interested in making life easier for their women. Mr. Khrushchev remarked that in the Soviet Union they did not have "the capitalist attitude toward women."

Nixon: "I think that this attitude toward women is universal. What we want to do is make easier the life of our housewives."

He explained that the house could be built for $14,000 and that most veterans had bought houses for between $10,000 and $15,000.

Nixon: "Let me give you an example you can appreciate. Our steel workers, as you know, are on strike.[3] But any steel worker could buy this house. They earn $3 an hour. This house costs about $100 a month to buy on a contract running twenty-five to thirty years."

Khrushchev: "We have steel workers and we have peasants who also can afford to spend $14,000 for a house." He said American houses were built to last only twenty years, so builders could sell new houses at the end of that period. "We build firmly. We build for our children and grandchildren."

Mr. Nixon said he thought American houses would last more than twenty years, but even so, after twenty years many Americans want a new home or a new kitchen, which would be obsolete then. The American

[3] For nearly four months in 1959, a half million members of the United Steelworkers of America engaged in one of the largest strikes in U.S. history, shutting down nearly every steel mill in the country. Workers sought better wages and job security in the face of corporate attempts to change work rules to reduce the number of employees.

system is designed to take advantage of new inventions and new techniques, he said.

Khrushchev: "This theory does not hold water."

He said some things never got out of date—furniture and furnishings, perhaps, but not houses. He said he did not think that what Americans had written about their houses was all strictly accurate.

Gadgetry Derided by Khrushchev

Nixon (pointing to television screen): "We can see here what is happening in other parts of the home."

Khrushchev: "This is probably always out of order."

Nixon: "Da [yes]."

Khrushchev: "Don't you have a machine that puts food into the mouth and pushes it down? Many things you've shown us are interesting but they are not needed in life. They have no useful purpose. They are merely gadgets. We have a saying, if you have bedbugs you have to catch one and pour boiling water into the ear."

Nixon: "We have another saying. This is that the way to kill a fly is to make it drink whisky. But we have a better use for whisky. [Aside] I like to have this battle of wits with the Chairman. He knows his business."

Khrushchev (manifesting a lack of interest in a dataprocessing machine that answers questions about the United States): "I have heard of your engineers. I am well aware of what they can do. You know for launching our missiles we need lots of calculating machines."

Nixon (hearing jazz music): "I don't like jazz music."

Khrushchev: "I don't like it either."

Nixon: "But my girls like it."

Mr. Nixon apologized for being "a poor host at the exposition and allowing a ceremonial visit to turn into a hot foreign policy discussion."

Mr. Khrushchev (apologizing): "I always speak frankly." He said he hoped he had not offended Mr. Nixon.

Nixon: "I've been insulted by experts. Everything we say is in good humor."

Russians Have It Too, Premier Asserts

Khrushchev: "The Americans have created their own image of the Soviet man and think he is as you want him to be. But he is not as you think. You think the Russian people will be dumbfounded to see these things, but the fact is that newly built Russian houses have all this

equipment right now. Moreover, all you have to do to get a h[c]
born in the Soviet Union. You are entitled to housing. I was born [in]
Soviet Union. So I have a right to a house. In America if you don't have a
dollar—you have the right to choose between sleeping in a house or on
the pavement. Yet you say that we are slaves of communism."

Nixon: "I appreciate that you are very articulate and energetic."

Khrushchev: "Energetic is not the same as wise."

Nixon: "If you were in our Senate, we would call you a filibusterer.
You do all the talking and don't let anyone else talk. To us, diversity, the
right to choose, the fact that we have 1,000 builders building 1,000 different houses, is the most important thing. We don't have one decision
made at the top by one government official. This is the difference."

Khrushchev: "On political problems we will never agree with you.
For instance, [First Deputy Premier] Mikovan likes very peppery soup.
I do not. But this does not mean that we do not get along."

Nixon: "You can learn from us and we can learn from you. There
must be a free exchange. Let the people choose the kind of house, the
kind of soup, the kind of ideas they want."

Mr. Khrushchev shifted the talk back to washing machines.

Nixon: "We have many different manufacturers and many different
kinds of washing machines so that the housewives have a choice."

U.S. Models Stop the Debate, Briefly

Khrushchev (noting Nixon gazing admiringly at young women model-
ing bathing suits and sports clothes): "You are for the girls too."

Nixon (indicating a floor sweeper that works by itself and other appliances): "You don't need a wife."

Khrushchev chuckled.

Nixon: "We do not claim to astonish the Russian people. We hope to
show our diversity and our right to choose. We do not wish to have decisions made at the top by government officials who say that all homes
should be built in the same way. Would it not be better to compete in the
relative merits of washing machines than in the strength of rockets. Is
this the kind of competition you want?"

Khrushchev: "Yes, that's the kind of competition we want. But your
generals say: 'Let's compete in rockets. We are strong and we can beat
you.' But in this respect we can also show you something."

Nixon: "To me you are strong and we are strong. In some ways, you
are stronger than we are. In others, we are stronger. We are both strong
not only from the standpoint of weapons but from the standpoint of will

and spirit. Neither should use that strength to put the other in a position where he in effect has an ultimatum. In this day and age that misses the point. With modern weapons it does not make any difference if war comes. We both have had it."

Khrushchev: "For the fourth time I have to say I cannot recognize my friend Mr. Nixon. If all Americans agree with you, then who don't we agree [with]? This is what we want."

Nixon: "Anyone who believes the American Government does not reflect the people is not an accurate observer of the American scene. I hope the Prime Minister understands all the implications of what I have just said. Whether you place either one of the powerful nations or any other in a position so that they have no choice but to accept dictation or fight, then you are playing with the most destructive force in the world.

"This is very important in the present world context. It is very dangerous. When we sit down at a conference table it cannot all be one way. One side cannot put an ultimatum to another. It is impossible. But I shall talk to you about this later."

Premier Insists That's a Threat

Khrushchev: "Who is raising an ultimatum?"

Nixon: "We will discuss that later."

Khrushchev: "If you have raised the question, why not go on with it now while the people are listening? We know something about politics, too. Let your correspondents compare watches and see who is filibustering. You put great emphasis on 'diktat' [dictation]. Our country has never been guided by 'diktat.' 'Diktat' is a foolish policy."

Nixon: "I am talking about it in the international sense."

Khrushchev: "It sounds to me like a threat. We, too, are giants. You want to threaten—we will answer threats with threats."

Nixon: "That's not my point. We will never engage in threats."

Khrushchev: "You wanted indirectly to threaten me. But we have the means to threaten too."

Nixon: "Who wants to threaten?"

Khrushchev: "You are talking about implications. I have not been. We have the means at our disposal. Ours are better than yours. It is you who want to compete. Da Da Da."

Nixon: "We are well aware of that. To me who is best is not material."

Khrushchev: "You raised the point. We want peace and friendship with all nations, especially with America."

Nixon: "We want peace too, and I believe that you do also."

Khrushchev: "Yes, I believe that."

Nixon: "I see that you want to build a good life. But I don't think that the cause of peace is helped by reminders that you have greater strength than us because that is a threat too."

Khrushchev: "I was answering your words. You challenged me. Let's argue fairly."

Nixon: "My point was that in today's world it is immaterial which of the two great countries at any particular moment has the advantage. In war, these advantages are illusory. Can we agree on that?"

Khrushchev: "Not quite. Let's not beat around the bush."

Nixon: "I like the way he talks."

6

YE. LITOSHKO

A Talk to the Point

July 25, 1959

As the official newspaper of the Soviet Communist Party and the primary publication for announcing government policies, Pravda *("Truth") was required reading for officials in the Soviet government, the military, and state-run companies. The newspaper provided a markedly different rendering of Nixon's and Khrushchev's discussion from the version presented in the Western press.*

Several hours before the U.S. National Exhibition opened yesterday in Moscow, it was visited by Soviet leaders. They looked over displays in the main pavilion and in the geodesic pavilion and tarried especially long in the so-called typical American home on exhibit at the fair. There Nikita Sergeyevich Khrushchev and U.S. Vice-President R. Nixon had a lively and frank talk.

N. S. Khrushchev, examining the kitchen of the American home, asked of what materials the kitchen equipment was made.

From Ye. Litoshko, "A Talk to the Point," *Pravda,* July 25, 1959, 1–2. Translated in *Current Digest of the Soviet Press* 11, no. 30: 3–4.

"Steel and aluminum," Nixon replied.

"I think it would be better and cheaper to use plastics."

The head of the Soviet government advised Nixon to acquaint himself with the way apartments are being built in Moscow's new apartment houses. If you do so, he said, you will see that our new kitchens are in no way inferior to yours.

Mr. Nixon declared that housewives' needs are considered in America.

"Still, we respect women more than the capitalist countries do," Comrade Khrushchev answered.

As the talk proceeded, N. S. Khrushchev stated that he was familiar with American construction technology although he had never been to the United States.

"The home you're showing is attractive, of course. But we won't build houses of this kind. They are made of plywood and won't last more than 20 years. This is not my opinion alone. Spokesmen of American building firms say so themselves. We ourselves at one time bought homes of this type from Finland, but we've stopped now because it's not profitable. Houses should be built solidly, out of reinforced concrete and brick, so that our children and grandchildren can live in them."

The U.S. Vice-President remarked that the grandchildren might have other tastes.

"Yes, that really can happen," said Nikita Sergeyevich. "Furniture can be changed, to be sure, but there's no point demolishing and burning the houses."

The conversation soon shifted to the manner in which American propaganda treats the Soviet people's way of life.

"Speaking about that, Mr. Nixon, I'd like to tell you an amusing Oriental story. A certain mullah was once walking down a road, and when he was asked where he was headed he replied, 'Over there, to that mountain. They say they're giving out free pilaf there.' A crowd of people rushed in the direction the mullah had indicated. When the mullah saw this, he himself believed his lie — 'Maybe they really are giving out free pilaf there?' — and he started to run with the others. The same with your propaganda," Nikita Sergeyevich concluded, to the friendly laughter of all those present. "You invented a fantastic image of Soviet man, and you have yourselves come to believe in your figment. Here you are showing your house and kitchen and thinking to amaze Soviet people with them. An American needs a lot of money to buy a house like that, and a Soviet man has the right to demand housing of the city Soviet chairman. As you know, our housing rent is very, very low. It's something of a token payment, if you please. You talk a great deal about your freedoms, but they also include the freedom to spend the night under a bridge."

This topic was evidently not to the liking of the American partner in the exchange. He preferred to take up the subject of washing machines, stating that it would be better to stress them and compete in their production rather than in the construction of rockets.

"I don't recognize you, Mr. Nixon," joked Comrade Khrushchev. "If you think the way you say you do, you and I could easily come to an understanding. It's your generals who are yelling about rockets and not kitchen utensils, it's they who are threatening us with rockets, it's they who are blustering that they can wipe us off the face of the earth. But this, of course, we shall permit no one to do. And to those who try we'll show the beetle's mother [*kuzkina mat*],[1] as we say in Russia."

Seasoned interpreters were hard put to it to translate this Russian expression into English. To the amusement of the bystanders, Nikita Sergeyevich had to correct Mr. Nixon's interpreter, who tried to render this idiomatic term "Kuzma's mother" [Kuzma is a Russian given name.—Trans.].

"We'll have more to say on that subject next time," declared Mr. Nixon, beating a hasty retreat.

"Why next time? Let's talk now," Nikita Sergeyevich insisted.

Vice-President Nixon expressed the wish that dictatorial methods and ultimatums not be employed in international relations, since they could force one side or the other to resort to war.

Comrade N. S. Khrushchev fully shared this point of view. As he indicated, however, the whole point was who actually was having recourse to dictation and ultimatums. Talk of war really did sound like a threat, he said.

"But threats don't work on us," N. S. Khrushchev warned, "and they never will. You won't succeed that way with us. You have a thing or two and we do, too, and better than yours in the bargain. Well, then, wouldn't it be better for us to be friends? We want to be friends with America and with all other countries. Then it's better that we drop talk of dictation and ultimatums. Let's not drag a dead cat by the tail."

The candid tone of the conversation, which was followed with great interest by Soviet and foreign correspondents as well as by many workers engaged in the construction of the American exhibition, evidently impressed Mr. Nixon too.

---

[1] A threatening expression from a colloquial vulgar Russian oath, "to show someone the beetle's mother."

"I like the way you talk," Nixon affirmed. "You'd be a good speaker in the States." . . .

At the end of the talk, N. S. Khrushchev stretched out his hand to the American attendant who had demonstrated the kitchen equipment.

"I thank you, little housewife, for so graciously allowing us to carry on this discussion in the kitchen."

At the exit of the "typical" American home, Nikita Sergeyevich pointed out two young Soviet workers to R. Nixon: "See what eagles they are? With eagles like these, it ill becomes our government to fear anyone's threats. Take a closer look at them. Do they look like slaves? Here you are holding a so-called Captive Nations Week in the United States. But what kind of slaves are these?"

"Nikita Sergeyevich, we've even forgotten the word and what it means," these fine, rosy-cheeked lads in exuberant health replied with a smile.

In turn, Mr. Nixon pointed to the tall, well-built young Americans standing with the Russians.

"What's wrong with our eagles?"

Nikita Sergeyevich at once replied: "Well, they must be friends. How much good they could accomplish together!"

The tour of the exhibition was over. N. S. Khrushchev and the other Soviet leaders shook hands with the Vice-President of the United States.

With stormy applause and acclaiming shouts, hundreds of workers and officials of the exhibition, as well as many correspondents, saw the Soviet leaders on their way and thanked N. S. Khrushchev for his frank talk.

7

V. OSIPOV

First Day, First Impressions
July 26, 1959

In this article, a Soviet journalist, likely pressured to present a government-approved response to the American National Exhibition, reports on the apparent disappointment experienced by some Soviet visitors. The article was published in Izvestia *("The News"), a widely read*

From V. Osipov, "First Day, First Impressions," *Izvestia*, July 26, 1959, 3. Translated in *Current Digest of the Soviet Press* 11, no. 30: 7–8.

Soviet newspaper that presented the official views of tl
ture. (In contrast, Pravda *was the Communist Party'*

A lightweight, gold-colored dome of anodized aluminum. ᴵ ·
masts in front of the entrance. The flag of the U.S.A. and the red flag ᴏ.
the Soviet Union flutter in the sunlight above the greenery of Sokolniki.
The U.S. National Exhibition had its official opening the day before yesterday, and yesterday thousands of visitors came out to it.

Muscovites had awaited the exhibition with interest, and understandably so. Our people know about the many great achievements of the
United States in industry and agriculture, and they have some idea of
American goods and their quality. American efficiency and high production standards are famous and highly esteemed here. People go to
Sokolniki with the idea that the U.S. National Exhibition will acquaint
them with the life of the American people, with the science that gave the
world Franklin and Salk and the culture that gave rise to Twain, London and Dreiser, and with their technology, with which our school children become familiar when they first hear the name of Thomas Edison.
Finally, they expected that the exhibition would broaden their picture of
America and of the intellectual world of the people who live there. And
now the exhibition has opened.

It is interesting to learn the visitors' first impressions. We approached
a Muscovite on his way out and asked: "What did you like best here?"
The elderly, gray-haired man (Yegor Merkulov by name) said:

"Well there are many interesting things here. I liked, for instance,
the—what do you call it?—the geodesic dome with its frame of prefabricated aluminum pipe. The main pavilion is beautiful, so light and trans-
parent. Many of the plastic goods, everyday and household articles, are
fine, and so are the bright colors of the fabrics. I liked the layout of the
apartment. My wife would probably have liked the kitchen utensils best,
and my son the shallow transistor television set. Other things at the
exhibition deserve attention too. But frankly, I expected more and, if
you'll pardon my saying so, I'm a little disappointed."

We approached a group of people. The badges on their jackets indicated that they were university graduates or graduate students. They
were engaged in a lively discussion of what they had seen.

"Our impressions? In general, it is all right. But you see," a tall, strong
fellow with glasses said, "you go from one photomural to another, from
one exhibit to another. All the time, you expect to see something to make
you stop and think, something that will help toward a deeper understanding of the United States and of that great country's people. With

ιι view, we even went back and made a second tour of the exhibits. ιour expectations are still unsatisfied and America is 'undiscovered.'"

A blonde girl interrupted her comrade: "You know, I keep asking myself: After all, is this the national exhibition of an immense country or the branch of a department store? Where is American science? Where is American production machinery, especially the plant machinery that we rightly hold in such high esteem? Can we really base our judgment of it on these lawn-mowers? Where is American culture? Ask this of the exhibition and you will get no answer."

We thanked these people and said goodby, while they went on talking about the exhibition, as they had been when interrupted by our intrusion.

8

VL. ZHUKOV

What the Facts Say

July 28, 1959

In this article from the Communist Party's official newspaper, Pravda, *a Soviet reporter critiques the American National Exhibition for not accurately representing the lot of the "average" American.*

"So much has been said and written about American prosperity that almost everywhere — both here in the United States and abroad — many people assume that every American owns a two-story house and a luxurious car, is well fed and clothed and enjoys medical care. However, a multitude of facts indicate that a great many manual workers have no idea of these material benefits, public health and leisure."

These words appeared in the American newspaper Washington Post and Times Herald. "Who are these people who are not shown in any motion picture or magazine that portrays life in the United States of America?" the newspaper asks, and it goes on to say that they are the

From Vl. Zhukov, "What the Facts Say," *Pravda*, July 28, 1959, 4. Translated in *Current Digest of the Soviet Press* 11, no. 30: 9–10.

workers and farmers, all those whose labor creates the material wealth of the country.

U.S. propagandists have a great deal to say about the high living standard of the "average American." But who is he, this "average American"?

To judge from statements of American government figures, it would seem that the person who comes closest to this ideal is the U.S. factory worker, who, they say, has a weekly income of about $90, or (at the rate of ten rubles to a dollar) 905 rubles 40 kopeks. It is asserted that such a wage is fully sufficient to live on in the U.S.A.

Is this true? We have before us the 14th U.S. "Labor Fact Book," which was prepared by the Labor Research Association. Let us turn to the data published in this book.

First of all, how does an American who receives $90 a week live? The answer to this question is provided by studies carried out by the A.F.L.-C.I.O., the American trade union association. According to its data, a family can live on $90 a week so long as it buys less than half a liter of milk; less than one egg per family member per day; makes no more than three telephone calls a week using a pay phone (a home phone is ruled out); and goes on vacation no more than once every three or four years.

Can the family even think of a television set, a five-room apartment and things like that if it must economize on such everyday foodstuffs as eggs and milk? A $90-a-week budget is barely sufficient to make ends meet.

This conclusion is supported by data from a survey made by the American company Peacock Publications. This survey shows that the family budget of an American who earns a little more—$100 a week— is about as follows: taxes and rent, $50.40 (504 rubles); transportation expenses, $10 (100 rubles). Thus taxes, rent and transportation consume more than 60% of the budget. The greater part of what is left goes for food.

What does this leave the family for other expenses? It can spend no more than $6.50 a week on clothing, $4.50 on medical care, $4.15 on entertainment of all kinds and $6 on other expenses. In a word, the "prospering" American family must save for two months in order to buy the cheapest man's suit, which costs $46.

The head of such a family cannot even dream of giving his children a higher education. After all, according to official studies a student's total expenses, including tuition, amount to $50 (500 rubles) a week.

Is it easy for such a family to buy such household articles as a refrigerator ($220.75, or 2207.5 rubles), a television set ($195.98, or 1959.8 rubles), an electric sewing machine ($180, or 1800 rubles) or a gas range ($173.80, or 1738 rubles)? These prices are taken from the American exhibition in Moscow.

Each year the Heller Committee for Research in Social Economics at the University of California compiles a budget for a family of four persons: husband and wife, a 13-year-old son and an eight-year-old daughter. This budget is widely recognized by U.S. scholars and politicians as typical for the whole country and as providing the "modest living standard" necessary for a "healthy and reasonably comfortable existence." The "Heller budget" published in September, 1958, called for $6087 a year, or $117 a week. In other words, the income of the "average" American industrial worker is far below what the Heller Committee considers a minimum.

9

Home Economist Demonstrates Convenience Foods

July 1959

The original USIA caption for this photograph states, "Russian visitors at the United States exhibition in Sokolniki Park see for themselves how typical United States housewives prepare a meal in a matter of minutes by using ready mixed products, and frozen foods. The home economists, speaking Russian, demonstrate how this can be done. They use the same type of kitchen appliances, and crockery used in millions of U.S. homes." USIA publicists distributed this photograph and caption to journalists to garner media attention for the exhibition. The two highly educated women who represented American housewives in Sokolniki Park were far from "typical," however. Marylee Duehring (pictured here) and Barbara Sampson were both full-time employees of major food-processing corporations (General Foods and General Mills, respectively) and had extensive media and public relations experience. Like typical American women, however, they did not speak Russian, despite the caption's erroneous claim. Rather, they relied on translators to communicate with Soviet fairgoers.

Image 59-14563, Box 2, Series PS-D, RG 306, National Archives II, College Park, Md.

Figure 1. *Home Economist Demonstrates Convenience Foods*

10

ROBERT LERNER

The Miracle Kitchen

March 1959

The following photograph shows home economist and women's magazine editor Anne Sonopol Anderson admiring the robotic floor cleaner of the RCA/Whirlpool Miracle Kitchen, one of three kitchens displayed at the American National Exhibition in Moscow. The Miracle Kitchen also included a push-button "electronic brain" command center, a remote-controlled mobile dishwasher, and automatically adjustable sinks.

Robert Lerner, photographer, LC-L901A-59-8225-2, *LOOK* Magazine Photograph Collection, Prints and Photographs Division, Library of Congress, Washington, D.C.

Figure 2. *The Miracle Kitchen*

11

Everything for Soviet Man

August 5, 1959

Several blocks away from the American National Exhibition, the Soviets erected their own exhibition, "Everything for Soviet Man." Intended to highlight the productivity of the Soviet economy, the exhibit included various consumer goods displays, such as this model of an ideal kitchen stocked with the latest USSR-made appliances and cookware.

Figure 3. *Kitchen Display at the "Everything for Soviet Man" Exhibition*

12

EDWARD L. FREERS

U.S. Diplomat's Telegram on the American National Exhibition

September 8, 1959

U.S. diplomat Edward L. Freers sent this telegram to the U.S. State Department, enthusiastically declaring the success of the American National Exhibition. In contrast to diplomat Llewellyn Thompson's secret telegram criticizing USIA planning for the exhibition (see Document 1), this telegram was marked "unclassified." Despite being addressed to the secretary of state, it was (as Freers expected) distributed widely to American diplomats in Washington.

IN FITTING CLIMAX TO FORTY-TWO HISTORY MAKING DAYS CROWDS ON CLOSING DAY OF AMERICAN EXHIBITION IN MOSCOW BROKE ALL PREVIOUS ATTENDANCE RECORDS. ESTIMATED 130,000 PEOPLE SURGED THROUGH EXHIBITIONS NINE ACRE SITE IN MOS-COWS BEAUTIFUL SOKOLNIKI PARK TO HAVE FINAL LOOK AT SHOW WHICH BECAME KNOWN ALL OVER USSR AND WAS SEEN BY MORE [THAN] TWO AND THREE QUAR-TERS MILLION SOVIET PEOPLE. PERHAPS GREATEST OVERALL MESSAGE EXHIBITION HAD IN THIS HIGHLY PLANNED COUNTRY WAS TO SHOW TREMENDOUS DIVERSITY OF AMERICAN LIFE, IDEAS, AND MANUFACTURES. NOWHERE WAS THIS MORE DRAMATI-CALLY EXEMPLIFIED THAN IN 400-FOOT CRESCENT-SHAPED GLASS PAVILION WHERE PRODUCTS OF HUNDREDS OF AMERICAN COMPANIES WERE DISPLAYED IN TWO STORY ALUMINIUM "JUNGLE GYM" ACCENTED WITH BRIGHT COLOR AND PHOTO MURALS. FACT THAT EXHIBITION WAS COOPERATIVE EFFORT OF GOVERNMENT AND PRIVATE ENTERPRISE NOT LOST ON VISITORS. . . .

ALL AGES FLOCKED TO CAR EXHIBIT BUT ACCORDING TO GUIDE GEORGE FEIFER NOBODY LOVED CARS LIKE GEORGIANS WHO WOULD MAKE BEE-LINE FOR AUTO SHOW

From Edward L. Freers, Telegram from Embassy in Moscow to Secretary of State, September 8, 1959, Folder 4, Box 4, RG 306 Entry 54, National Archives II, College Park, Md.

[FROM] ENTRY GATE AND STAY THERE ALL DAY. NEXT IN POPULARITY WERE CULTURAL PRESENTATIONS — WALT DISNEYS 360 DEGREE FILM, CIRCARAMA, EDWARD STECHENS PHOTO ESSAY "THE FAMILY OF MAN" AND CHARLES EAMES SEVEN-SCREEN FILM ON AMERICAN LIFE. ANOTHER AND ONE OF MOST IMPORTANT CULTURAL FEATURES OF EXHIBITION WAS SERIES OF CONCERTS GIVEN BY NEW YORK PHILHARMONIC SYMPHONY ORCHESTRA UNDER DIRECTION OF LEONARD BERNSTEIN. ALL OF BERNSTEIN CONCERTS RECEIVED TREMENDOUS OVATIONS AND HIGHLY ENTHUSIASTIC PLAUDITS FROM THE PRESS. IZVESTIYA REPORTED: WONDEROUS ENSEMBLE, AUDIENCES CAPTIVATED. INTEREST IN ALL EXHIBITS FROM SMALLEST TOY TO LARGE WHEAT COMBINE TREMENDOUS. ALL DISPLAYS CROWDED WITH PEOPLE DURING ENTIRE RUN OF EXHIBITION. PROBABLY NO ONE MORE DELIGHTED WITH AMERICAN EXHIBITION THAN SOVIET WOMEN. "WE HAVE NEVER SEEN SUCH WAY TO SHOW CLOTHES," EXCLAIMED SOVIET SALESGIRL. "WE SEE NOT ONLY CLOTHES BUT THROUGH YOUR MUSIC AND PANTOMIME UNDERSTAND AMERICAN WAY OF LIFE." GIRLS IN DUDE RANCH OUTFITS AND WEDDING SCENE ALWAYS BROUGHT EXCLAMATIONS AND FREQUENTLY APPLAUSE FROM AUDIENCE. FOUR KITCHENS WHIRLPOOLS ELECTRONICALLY CONTROLLED KITCHEN OF FUTURE, GENERAL FOODS-GENERAL MILLS KITCHEN WHERE CONVENIENCE FOODS WERE DEMONSTRATED, WESTINGHOUSE KITCHEN IN MODEL APARTMENT, AND GENERAL ELECTRIC KITCHEN IN MODEL HOUSE WERE JAMMED WITH ADMIRING SOVIET WOMEN FROM MORNING UNTIL NIGHT. EVEN AFTER LIGHTS WENT OUT AT NIGHT THEY STOOD NEAR KITCHEN ASKING QUESTIONS OF DEMONSTRATORS. MEN INTERESTED TOO. ENGINEER SO CURIOUS ABOUT WESTINGHOUSE TOASTER HE BROUGHT LOAF BREAD TO SEE HOW IT WORKED WITH SOVIET PRODUCT. BIRDSEYE FROZEN FOODS AND GENERAL MILLS MIXES DEMONSTRATED BY BARBARA SAMPSON AND MARYLEE DUERHING OF KEEN INTEREST NOT ONLY TO HOUSEWIVES BUT SOVIET FOOD PROCESSORS. TWO SINGER EXHIBITS ON INDUSTRIAL AND HOME SEWING MACHINES IN ACTION STAFFED WITH RUSSIAN PACKING OPERATORS WERE OF INTENSE INTEREST TO SOVIET WOMEN MANY OF WHOM EITHER MAKE OWN CLOTHES OR HAVE THEM MADE. . . .

AS THEY LEFT EXHIBITION SOVIET VISITORS TOOK WITH THEM NOT ONLY MEMORY OF DAY SPENT "IN AMERICA" BUT MORE THAN FIFTEEN MILLION COPIES OF MORE THAN SCORE OF PAMPHLETS CONTRIBUTED BY AMERICAN FIRMS DEALING WITH VARIED ASPECTS OF AMERICAN LIFE AND MANY OF PRODUCTS DISPLAYED. SO GREAT WAS DEMAND FOR LITERATURE THAT SERIOUS CROWD CONTROL PROBLEMS CAUSED BY DISTRIBUTION OF SOME BROCHURES PARTICULARLY THOSE ON AUTOMOBILES. MANY TIMES DURING EXHIBITION KHRUSHCHEV DECLARED SOVIET UNION WOULD OVERTAKE AND PASS UNITED STATES IN PRODUCTION. IN REFERENCE TO THIS ONE SOVIET VISITOR WROTE: "IF EXHIBITION REPRESENTS AMERICAN WAY OF LIFE THEN IT IS AMERICAN WAY OF LIFE WE SHOULD OVERTAKE." OR AS ANOTHER SAID AFTER SEEING EXHIBITION: "JUST LET ME OFF AT AMERICA AS WE GO BY." . . .

FREERS

13

Favorable Comments on Exhibition
September 1959

Soviet visitors were invited to write down their reactions to the American National Exhibition. Whether the comments marked by USIA officials as "favorable" (in this document) or as "unfavorable" (in Document 14) were genuine is difficult to know, as some of the visitors to Sokolniki Park were volunteers specially prepped by Communist Party officials to publicly challenge American propaganda.

Thank you for the Exhibition. It realizes well its basic aim of improving mutual understanding between our nations. (Unsigned)

The American Exhibition convincingly shows that private enterprise produces more and in stupendous quantities the very best goods in the world. Greetings and best wishes to the cleverest American people. (Illegible, an electrician) . . .

Okay, Yankees! Some day we will catch up with you in all areas where we lag behind. But in general we wish you well and would like to hear the same from you addressed to us. (Signature illegible) . . .

I am sixty-four years old and I am very glad I lived until I could personally visit the American National Exhibition for which I thank its initiators from the bottom of my heart. I am a small man and I particularly liked the spirit of the following exhibits: circarama, geodesic dome, and Family of Man. I am also grateful for the pepsi-cola. I thank you twice. (Signature illegible, a pensioner)

There are many beautiful things at your Exhibition-building, machinery, photographs—miracle of miracles—and many other articles. The Exhibition gave us a chance to learn about people and life in America. We thank your President and the organizers of the Exhibition. (University teacher)

From "Favorable Comments on Exhibition," n.d. (September 1959), Folder 4, Box 4, RG 306 Entry 54, National Archives II, College Park, Md.

14

Unfavorable Comments on Exhibition
September 1959

Many Soviet visitors wrote negative comments about the American National Exhibition. The themes presented in these selections were commonly repeated, suggesting that at least some visitors were coached beforehand to question the exhibition.

General

The Exhibition does not give anything to the mind not to the soul. It looks like a haberdashery store. There are more sofa cushions than things which might please us and let us understand what kind of people Americans are. (Illegible)

The Exhibition does not impress me. It resembles an advertisement more than an exhibition of a country which is a leader in the area of technology. An impression that America is more interested in looking after its comforts and amusements rather than after the spiritual enrichment of man is created. (A. Belova)

Leaving the Exhibition I carry with me an impression of glittering metal saucepans. (Illegible)

I had an impression that I had visited a factory of half-finished materials. (A visitor)

Lack of Industrial and Technological Exhibits

We think that a country which has existed without wars and destruction for about two centuries could show greater achievements in technology, science, culture and even everyday living. Is it possible to consider kitchens and cosmetics as a cult of man? (A group of visitors)

From "Unfavorable Comments on Exhibition," n.d. (September 1959), Folder 4, Box 4, RG 306 Entry 54, National Archives II, College Park, Md.

I expected more and I am disappointed. Is it possible that you think our mental outlook is restricted to everyday living only? There is too little technology. Where is your industry?

We expected that the American Exhibition would show something grandiose, something similar to Soviet sputniks . . . and you Americans want to surprise us with the glitter of your kitchen pans and the fashions which do not appeal to us at all. (Unsigned) . . .

Typical House

Having seen the typical house of an American family, I decided to write my impressions. Yes, it is a typical little house of an American family of Browns. Poor little house! During 12 days of your existence more was said about you than any other exhibit here. People began talking about you before you were brought to our country. There you were criticized because you were too expensive and because you were not typical of American conditions where thousands of families were cooped up in slums and it was laughable for them to hear that you were typical. We saw your slums with our own eyes because we lived there several years. We know well the Italian and Latin blocks and Chinatown and even visited Harlem once in daylight, though apprehensively, because we could have been taken for Americans and killed by mistake. So if Americans laughed, and apparently they had reasons, we Russians say: "All this unquestionably is very nice. Thank you, Americans for trying to show us Russians what houses should be built and how to furnish them. Many thanks, but such light-weight buildings do not please us and do not foist on us your manner of living." (Gorokhova, Davydova, Semnova)

15

YE. LITOSHKO

On Nixon's Visit to the Urals

July 31, 1959

In this article from the Communist Party's official newspaper, Pravda, *a staff reporter documents how Soviet guides sought to impress Nixon with their country's industrial productivity and the consumer comforts provided under socialism as he toured sites outside Moscow.*

Sverdlovsk, July 30—The American guests, headed by U.S. Vice-President R. Nixon, have spent their second day here acquainting themselves with the wealth of the celebrated Urals region, its achievements and its people. And the Urals workers really have something to show the foreign guests. Yesterday Mr. Nixon spent more than two hours in the shops of the Urals Machine-Building Plant—"the plant of plants," in A. M. Gorky's[1] apt phrase.

"All this is magnificent, remarkable, splendid!" the U.S. Vice-President and his companions exclaimed as they looked over the operation of this gigantic enterprise.

Today the same kind of enthusiastic comments could be heard in the shops of the Pervouralsk New Pipe Plant near Sverdlovsk. R. Nixon said:

"Your plant is very modern, very efficient and productive."

After the guests had looked over the plant, they visited the Palace of Culture. On leaving this building, R. Nixon chatted with a group of local residents.

"I heard some of you say the word 'peace' in English," he remarked. "I want to answer you in Russian: Druzya, za mir vo vsem mire! [Friends, for peace throughout the world!]"

---

[1]A founder of the socialist realist literary movement, Aleksey Maksimovich Gorky (1868–1936) was one of Russia's and the Soviet Union's most famous writers.

From Ye. Litoshko, "'Back Up Words about Peace with Deeds,' Urals Workers Tell U.S. Vice-President," *Pravda*, July 31, 1959, 4. Translated in *Current Digest of the Soviet Press* 11, no. 31: 7.

"A few more deeds!" one worker suggested.

Then the guests left for the copper mine in Degtyarsk. . . .

The guests visited the dispatching point. The following exchange took place between the Vice-President and A. P. Orlov, a dispatcher.

"You look much younger than your age," R. Nixon remarked. "You must live well?"

"All of us live well," A. P. Orlov replied.

The elderly dispatcher's words weren't even tinged with boasting. Many miners here earn 3000 rubles and more a month. They live in well-built homes and enjoy the benefits of culture. Degtyarsk has 17 schools and 12 kindergartens and a splendid Palace of Culture. Indeed, even New York's best Broadway theater companies would envy this building and its excellent facilities. In this Palace of Culture alone, 14 amateur art groups practice and perfect their artistic skills. There are a large reading room and an extensive library here. Mrs. Nixon, wife of the U.S. Vice-President; Vice-Admiral H. Rickover; and R. Dowling, the well-known American banker and patron of the arts, pleasurably spent more than an hour in this building. Miners and their children demonstrated their artistic skills for the guests.

"A wonderful performance. Very good," Mrs. Nixon said after this impromptu show. . . .

The American guests expressed a desire to see miners' homes. They dropped in at the apartment of Anatoly Kalyagin, a cutter. The housewife of the family was a bit flustered at the unexpected visit, but she was nevertheless happy to see the guests. She showed them her spotless, comfortable apartment, consisting of living room, bedroom and kitchen, and introduced her three-year-old daughter Olya to Mrs. Nixon, Dr. Milton Eisenhower and the other guests. The brother of the U.S. President noticed a television set in the corner and asked Comrade Kalyagin how much he earned at the mine.

"Between 3000 and 3500 rubles a month," the young miner answered.

"We have fine living conditions," the housewife told the guests. "My husband earns a good living, and we are fully provided with everything we need."

In the evening the guests returned to Sverdlovsk.

16

BILL MAULDIN

Boy, Did He Tell Them *Off!*

July 26, 1959

---

*Bill Mauldin was one of the most popular and critically acclaimed politi-
cal cartoonists of the mid-twentieth century. First published in the* St.
Louis Post-Dispatch, *the following pictorial commentary on Nixon's performance in Moscow, depicts the vice president strolling confidently out of
the Red Square tombs of former Soviet leaders Vladimir Lenin and Joseph
Stalin. (In 1961, Stalin's body was removed from Lenin's tomb under the
orders of Nikita Khrushchev.) Many political commentators would later
credit Nixon's strong performance with helping him secure the Republican nomination as presidential candidate in the 1960 U.S. election.*

Bill Mauldin, "Boy, Did He Tell Them Off," July 26, 1959, Bill Mauldin Papers, Library of
Congress, Washington, D.C.

Figure 4. *Boy, Did He Tell* Them *Off!*
Copyright by Bill Mauldin (1959). Courtesy of the Bill Mauldin Estate LLC.

17

NIKITA KHRUSHCHEV

Speech in Dnepropetrovsk

July 28, 1959

Speaking to a group of machine workers just days after the Kitchen Debate, Khrushchev trumpeted his efforts to convince Nixon as well as Soviet citizens that the Soviet Union was well on its way to winning the "peaceful competition" between capitalism and socialism. As was customary with all the premier's speeches, a transcript quickly appeared in Pravda, *the Communist Party's official newspaper.*

Dear comrades! On behalf of the Party Central Committee, the U.S.S.R. Council of Ministers and the Presidium of the U.S.S.R. Supreme Soviet, permit me to greet you heartily and to felicitate all the men and women workers, engineers and technicians and the entire collective of the plant on your successes in the drive to meet state plans ahead of schedule and to achieve technical progress. (*Stormy applause.*) . . .

Yes, our great and hard-working people do have imposing successes to their credit. They have literally staggered the world with their victories.

Wonderful results have also been achieved in the past few years in the upsurge of agriculture. Grain output has risen appreciably and we now have enough bread, both black and white. Is that right or isn't it?

Voices. Right!

N. S. Khrushchev. Do you have vegetables?

Voices. We do!

N. S. Khrushchev. Comrade Gayevoi, secretary of the province Party committee, is with us here. Are you perhaps saying this so you won't let him down, or do you really have enough vegetables?

Voices. We do have vegetables. Lots of vegetables!

N. S. Khrushchev. Do you have milk?

Voices. We do!

From Nikita Khrushchev, "Speech in Dnepropetrovsk," *Pravda*, July 30, 1959, 1–2. Translated in *Current Digest of the Soviet Press* 11, no. 30: 13–16.

N. S. Khrushchev: Do you have meat?

Voices. Yes, but still not enough!

N. S. Khrushchev. You have milk, but when it comes to meat opinions are divided. In the past several years the output of meat in our country has increased greatly. Meat production and purchases are rising sharply this year. As of July 20, meat procurements were 50% higher than on the same date last year.

That's something, isn't it, comrades?

Voices. It is indeed!

N. S. Khrushchev. Of course it is. But we still don't have enough meat. We've got to produce more. In response to the appeal of advanced collective and state farms, a movement has developed in the country to overtake and surpass the United States of America in the next few years in the per capita output of meat, milk and butter. In 1958 the U.S. produced 94 kg. of meat per capita. But a great deal of this meat was for export, so the country's actual per capita consumption is considerably less than that. We must also produce more milk, meat and other foodstuffs to satisfy the needs of Soviet people fully. We are confident that we shall meet our goal of overtaking the United States in meat, milk and butter output in the next few years. We have every prospect of doing so.

The Party and the government are directing their efforts to the speedier development of industry and agriculture and the improvement of the people's life. Our people are now living better than they did, and we're positive that they will live even better from now on.

Voices. Right!

N. S. Khrushchev. Far more consumer goods are now being turned out, and they are of better quality. But this is only the beginning. . . .

You know that the Vice-President of the United States, Mr. Nixon, is at present in the Soviet Union. He was commissioned by Mr. Eisenhower, President of the United States, to inaugurate the American exhibition in Moscow. We welcomed Vice-President Nixon's coming to the Soviet Union; we have greeted him fittingly, as protocol requires when such a distinguished guest is received and as befits the position he occupies in the United States.

We have had talks with Mr. Nixon. The U.S. Vice-President said, "We're for peace." I replied, "We believe that the American people also want peace. But if the Soviet people and the American people are for peace, why shouldn't we get together on improving relations between our countries in the interests of strengthening peace all over the world?"

I then asked Mr. Nixon, "If you're for peace, why have you taken such an unwise decision as to observe a so-called 'Captive Nations

Week'?" I put the question bluntly: "What do you want—to liberate our peoples from the 'slavery of communism'? Can you seriously consider the peoples of the socialist countries captive peoples?" (*Laughter.*)

On Sunday Mr. Nixon and I met out of town. I suggested to him: "Mr. Nixon, let's go to the Moscow River and see how the 'slaves of communism' relax." (*Laughter.*)

He accepted the suggestion, and we took a trip down the river together in a launch. Of course there are lots of people on the Moscow River, as there are here on the Dnieper. They go bathing, relax and have a good time on the shore.

We said to the U.S. Vice-President, "Take a look; these are the 'slaves of communism'!" (*Laughter.*)

Our launch approached the shore and at once many people gathered around. I asked how many present had a higher or secondary education. It turned out almost all of them did. "Here," I said, are 'slaves of communism, with higher and secondary educations. You say we're the slaves of communism while we consider you the slaves of capitalism. You don't understand simple things—that the age of capitalism is on the wane. But in our country even the Young Pioneers[1] understand that.

"Mr. Vice-President," I said further in my talk with Mr. Nixon, "we may think differently and have varying political opinions, but we have to live on the same planet. The only intelligent policy, therefore, is a policy of peaceful coexistence, a policy of ensuring peace among peoples. Let's wage a peaceful competition, let's have a contest to see which provides more material and spiritual boons for man—socialism or capitalism. The system that provides more benefits for the people will be the one that proves it is the best social order. Your system has been in existence for centuries. It's more than 180 years since you liberated yourselves from colonial bondage, while our Soviet state has existed 42 years in all, and already we're hard on your heels. So our system provides for the more rapid development of society on the road of progress."

The strength of our system is that it's a genuine people's system. Everything is decided in our society by those who create the material and spiritual blessings, and not by those who live off some one else's labor, not by capitalists, not by monopolists, not by millionaires and billionaires. That is the foundation of foundations of the stability and invincibility of our system and of its great creative force. We may at present still be lacking a thing or two and may in some respects be lagging

---

[1] The Young Pioneer Organization of the Soviet Union was a communist educational and recreational group for youth aged ten to fifteen.

.e United States. But, Messrs. Capitalists, even you are now ...o deny that the Soviet Union and its peoples have by their own ...s and in defiance of your intrigues achieved marvelous victories tha. have staggered the whole world. (*Applause.*)

We have a different social and political system than the capitalist countries, but is that any reason for war? It is not. After all, if we win out in the peaceful competition, no one stands to suffer from it—neither Americans, Englishmen, Frenchmen nor Germans—because this peaceful competition is a competition to increase production and develop the economy. This is a competition to see who provides the people with a better diet, better clothing, better shoes, who provides the people with better cultural living conditions. Let us compete in peacetime pursuits. That is noble. If you have confidence in your system, prove it. As for us, we're confident of the advantages of the socialist system, and we'll be on the advance. (*Applause.*)

2

Consumers and Consensus

The mass consumption on display at the American National Exhibition was widely understood to be crucial to the unprecedented prosperity of the post–World War II economy of the United States. While many influential social critics publicly worried that America's love affair with ranch-style homes, chrome-covered automobiles, overflowing super-markets, and shiny kitchen appliances signaled a crassly materialistic culture, other influential policymakers and social theorists celebrated mass consumption as a means to economic growth, full employment, high wages, and steady corporate profits. During the war, President Franklin Roosevelt had famously listed "freedom from want" alongside freedom of speech, freedom from fear, and freedom of worship as the "four freedoms" that defined America's mission in the world. After the war, liberals agreed that mass consumption, abetted by government policies and labor unions, was indeed key to making the American economy both more productive and more egalitarian.

The act of consumption was likewise essential for postwar communist states such as the Soviet Union, which continued to rely on a centralized command economy in which nearly all core economic decisions were dictated by Kremlin policies. As Soviet leaders sought to pull the country out of the devastation of World War II, promises of abundant consumer goods became more crucial for legitimizing the socialist project and the one-party rule of the Communists. When Nikita Khrushchev rose to power in 1953, he began promoting economic reforms aimed at increasing the production of consumer goods. The Soviet economy indeed grew remarkably quickly in the 1950s, outpacing every other industrialized nation (including the United States). As a consequence, many Soviet workers gained unprecedented access to foodstuffs, automobiles, housing, and other basic consumer goods. Seven months before the Kitchen Debate, Khrushchev unveiled a detailed seven-year economic plan that called for marked increases in the production of consumer goods. The 1959 economic plan and its promise of imminent socialist abundance were clearly on the minds of both Soviet and American observers when Richard Nixon arrived at Sokolniki Park. Just like American citizens, however, Soviets in the 1950s displayed ambivalence, expressing both hopes and fears about the cultural implications of an economy so devoted to mass consumption.

Capitalist Consumer Citizens

18

ALEX HENDERSON

Why We Eat Better

November 1951

This picture was taken for a photo-essay in a magazine for employees of the DuPont corporation, a chemical company that was one of the nation's largest businesses at the time. A DuPont employee and his family are depicted in a cold storage warehouse surrounded by two and a half tons of food, representing the estimated yearly diet of an average middle-class American family. The article accompanying the photograph suggested that the American dream of consumer abundance and upward mobility was due to corporate command of the industrial technology that enabled high worker wages. Additional images showed the same family surrounded by much less impressive piles of food estimated to be consumed by families in England, Belgium, West Germany, Poland, and China, providing a stark visual representation of American food abundance.

From Alex Henderson, "Why We Eat Better," *Better Living* magazine Picture File, ID 1972341_001, Hagley Museum and Library, Wilmington, Del.

Figure 5. *Why We Eat Better*

19

JOHN A. LOGAN

Speech on Modern Food Distribution
October 20, 1958

In the 1950s, John A. Logan led the National Association of Food Chains, a trade group representing America's supermarket chains. In this speech, delivered to a group of business executives and government experts, Logan suggested that modern methods of food retailing and distribution were transforming American consumer culture, creating a new form of "economic democracy."

Historians of the future may well call the twentieth century the Age of Distribution. Today's textbooks cite the introduction of agriculture and the Industrial Revolution as fundamental to the development of civilization as we know it in America today. So, young people of the future may find school classes devoted to the ways the revolution in distribution made it possible for the people of the twentieth century to learn to live peacefully in the atomic age. Distribution has made startling progress in the past forty years in America. . . .

The opportunity for mass distribution to become a reality was created by the introduction of the self-service principle. Hence, one of the most important dates in the history of distribution was 1916 when Clarence Saunders opened the first self-service food store in Memphis, Tennessee. This date ranks in importance with the development of canning, mechanical refrigeration, or the substitution of tractors for horses. It now is estimated that about 90 percent of grocery sales in the United States are by self-service. And the sales of perishable food products such as meat, fruits, vegetables, and dairy products are continuing rapidly to be converted to self-service methods with an estimated 60% sold through self-service today.

Why was—and is—self-service crucially important to mass distribution?

From John A. Logan, "Modern Food Distribution—Symbol of the American Way of Life," talk before the Boston Conference on Food Distribution, October 20, 1958, Food Marketing Institute Archives, Arlington, Va.

First, because of its effect on cost. Second, because it stimulated competition, setting in motion forces which paved the way toward other efficiencies in handling food and accelerated the rise of the supermarket.

Among other influences of self-service which are equally important and far-reaching are:

1) The stimulating effect on the demand for food. Self-service, through its invitation to "impulse" purchases, had an impact on the American food standard of living. The freedom to touch, see, smell, and feel merchandise increases sales and, as a result, food consumption is increased. This broadens markets for farm food products and helps create additional jobs all along the line from farm to table. Larger sales also reduce costs and allow lower prices which, in turn, increase food purchasing power.

2) A revolution in packaging resulting in more sanitary, easily handled products. The great development in the packaging and canning industries as we know them today was hastened by self-service. And improvement in standardization of quality and quantity of the products inside the packages became essential when self-service was introduced to obtain repeat sales. The package and the can had to become "silent salesmen" for their products to compete for consumer attention in self-service.

3) Inauguration of one-price merchandise with the price marked on each item and the same price to all customers. Self-service is such a potent idea that it has spread to other forms of retailing such as the variety store, drug store, hardware store and, more recently, the department store.

Aside from its purely economic effects in terms of cost of distributing food and increasing food consumption, self-service is a form of economic democracy. The consumer has free, unhampered choice. She can vote for the store she prefers to shop in, the different food items she wants, and for brands of her own choice. She is on her own, with no one to influence her or interfere with her freedom of choice. By her patronage, she has demonstrated that she likes the self-service way of life.

20

JOHN KENNETH GALBRAITH

The Affluent Society

1958

One of many public intellectuals concerned with the effects of American mass consumption, John Kenneth Galbraith was the most visible economist of his era. A liberal Keynesian, Galbraith insisted that the economy required government management to achieve full employment and maximum output. Galbraith also followed John Maynard Keynes's example in his attempts to educate and persuade a nonprofessional audience. In The Affluent Society, *Galbraith analyzed the weaknesses and injustices of an economy premised mainly on the profit-driven stimulation of consumer demand. The following passage, which explains how unrestrained private consumption undermines the provision of public goods, takes direct aim at the buoyant philosophy of "consumer choice" that so influenced Richard Nixon's remarks at the American Exhibition.* The Affluent Society *became a bestseller in 1958 and has never gone out of print.*

The Theory of Social Balance

The final problem of the productive society is what it produces. This manifests itself in an implacable tendency to provide an opulent supply of some things and a niggardly yield of others. This disparity carries to the point where it is a cause of social discomfort and social unhealth. The line which divides our area of wealth from our area of poverty is roughly that which divides privately produced and marketed goods and services from publicly rendered services. Our wealth in the first is not only in startling contrast with the meagerness of the latter, but our wealth in privately produced goods is, to a marked degree, the cause of crisis in the supply of public services. For we have failed to see the importance, indeed the urgent need, of maintaining a balance between the two.

This disparity between our flow of private and public goods and services is no matter of subjective judgment. On the contrary, it is the

From John Kenneth Galbraith, *The Affluent Society* (Boston: Houghton Mifflin, 1958), 251–61.

source of the most extensive comment which only stops short of the direct contrast being made here. In the years following World War II, the papers of any major city—those of New York were an excellent example—told daily of the shortages and shortcomings in the elementary municipal and metropolitan services. The schools were old and overcrowded. The police force was under strength and underpaid. The parks and playgrounds were insufficient. Streets and empty lots were filthy, and the sanitation staff was underequipped and in need of men. Access to the city by those who work there was uncertain and painful and becoming more so. Internal transportation was overcrowded, unhealthful, and dirty. So was the air. Parking on the streets had to be prohibited, and there was no space elsewhere. These deficiencies were not in new and novel services but in old and established ones. Cities have long swept their streets, helped their people move around, educated them, kept order, and provided horse rails for vehicles which sought to pause. That their residents should have a nontoxic supply of air suggests no revolutionary dalliance with socialism.

The discussion of this public poverty competed, on the whole successfully, with the stories of ever-increasing opulence in privately produced goods. The Gross National Product was rising. So were retail sales. So was personal income. Labor productivity had also advanced. The automobiles that could not be parked were being produced at an expanded rate. The children, though without schools, subject in the playgrounds to the affectionate interest of adults with odd tastes, and disposed to increasingly imaginative forms of delinquency, were admirably equipped with television sets. We had difficulty finding storage space for the great surpluses of food despite a national disposition to obesity. Food was grown and packaged under private auspices. The care and refreshment of the mind, in contrast with the stomach, was principally in the public domain. Our colleges and universities were severely overcrowded and underprovided, and the same was true of the mental hospitals.

The contrast was and remains evident not alone to those who read. The family which takes its mauve and cerise, air-conditioned, power-steered, and power-braked automobile out for a tour passes through cities that are badly paved, made hideous by litter, blighted buildings, billboards, and posts for wires that should long since have been put underground. They pass on into a countryside that has been rendered largely invisible by commercial art. (The goods which the latter advertise have an absolute priority in our value system. Such aesthetic considerations as a view of the countryside accordingly come second. On such matters we are consistent.) They picnic on exquisitely packaged food from a portable icebox by a polluted stream and go on to spend the night at a park which is a menace to public health and morals. Just before dozing off on an air mattress, beneath a nylon tent, amid the stench of decaying refuse, they may reflect vaguely on the curious unevenness of their blessings. Is this, indeed, the American genius? . . .

The case for social balance has, so far, been put negatively. Failure to keep public services in minimal relation to private production and use of goods is a cause of social disorder or impairs economic performance. The matter may now be put affirmatively. By failing to exploit the opportunity to expand public production we are missing opportunities for enjoyment which otherwise we might have had. Presumably a community can be as well rewarded by buying better schools or better parks as by buying bigger automobiles. By concentrating on the latter rather than the former it is failing to maximize its satisfactions. As with schools in the community, so with public services over the country at large. It is scarcely sensible that we should satisfy our wants in private goods with reckless abundance, while in the case of public goods, on the evidence of the eye, we practice extreme self-denial. So, far from systematically exploiting the opportunities to derive use and pleasure from these services, we do not supply what would keep us out of trouble.

The conventional wisdom holds that the community, large or small, makes a decision as to how much it will devote to its public services. This decision is arrived at by democratic process. Subject to the imperfections and uncertainties of democracy, people decide how much of their private income and goods they will surrender in order to have public services of which they are in greater need. Thus there is a balance, however rough, in the enjoyments to be had from private goods and services and those rendered by public authority.

It will be obvious, however, that this view depends on the notion of independently determined consumer wants. In such a world one could with some reason defend the doctrine that the consumer, as a voter, makes an independent choice between public and private goods. But given the dependence effect—given that consumer wants are created by the process by which they are satisfied—the consumer makes no such choice. He is subject to the forces of advertising and emulation by which production creates its own demand. Advertising operates exclusively, and emulation mainly, on behalf of privately produced goods and services. Since management and emulative effects operate on behalf of private production, public services will have an inherent tendency to lag behind. Automobile demand which is expensively synthesized will inevitably have a much larger claim on income than parks or public health or even roads where no such influence operates. The engines of mass communication, in their highest state of development, assail the eyes and ears of the community on behalf of more beer but not of more schools. Even in the conventional wisdom it will scarcely be contended that this leads to an equal choice between the two.

The competition is especially unequal for new products and services. Every corner of the public psyche is canvassed by some of the nation's most talented citizens to see if the desire for some merchantable product can be cultivated. No similar process operates on behalf of the non-merchantable services of the state. Indeed, while we take the cultivation of new private wants for granted we would be measurably shocked to see it applied to public services. The scientist or engineer or advertising man who devotes himself to developing a new carburetor, cleanser, or depilatory for which the public recognizes no need and will feel none until an advertising campaign arouses it, is one of the valued members of our society. A politician or a public servant who dreams up a new public service is a wastrel. Few public offenses are more reprehensible.

So much for the influences which operate on the decision between public and private production. The calm decision between public and private consumption pictured by the conventional wisdom is, in fact, a remarkable example of the error which arises from viewing social behavior out of context. The inherent tendency will always be for public services to fall behind private production.

21

HERBLOCK

Split-Level Living
March 9, 1960

Herbert Block drew editorial cartoons for the Washington Post *for more than fifty years, from 1945 to 2001. The liberal sympathies of "Herblock" endeared him to some and enraged others. Echoing themes from Galbraith's* Affluent Society *(see Document 20), the following cartoon asks its viewers to consider the structural and moral weaknesses of American consumer society.*

Herbert Lawrence Block, "Split-Level Living," *Washington Post*, March 9, 1960.

Figure 6. *Split-Level Living*

22

EDMUND NASH

Report on Purchasing Power of Soviet Workers
1953

U.S. Information Agency officials drew the following statistical analysis from a report by Bureau of Labor Statistics agent Edmund Nash. The report focused on the challenges Soviet consumers faced in securing desired foodstuffs.

Real earnings of the average worker in the U.S.S.R. in 1953, in terms of food-buying power, were considerably below the 1928 level when a certain amount of free enterprise prevailed under the New Economic Policy (the NEP)[1] and peasants had not yet been forced into collective farms.[2] This comparison is the more striking in the light of the price cut of April 1953 and other official price cuts in recent years. The year 1928 appears to have marked the high point in Soviet real earnings, for toward its end

---

[1] The New Economic Policy of 1921–1928 was promoted by the Soviet Union's first leader, Vladimir Lenin, as a form of "state capitalism" that would provide some private market incentives to certain small business owners and agricultural producers.

[2] Joseph Stalin, after taking the helm of the Soviet Union in 1928, sought to radically transform Soviet agriculture by creating *kolkhozy*, or collective farms. Theoretically organized as "voluntary" cooperatives that pooled the labor of rural workers on giant farms managed by technocratic experts, Stalin's plan for collectivization was intended to boost food and fiber production to supply the needs of urban industrial workers. In practice, collectivization was usually forced upon farmworkers, and from 1928 to 1940 the campaign resulted in dramatic social and economic costs. Many peasants came to view the collectivization drive as an attempt to return them to czarist-era serfdom.

From Edmund Nash, "Purchasing Power of Soviet Workers, 1953," August 1953, Feature Packets, Recurring Subjects, Box 7, RG 306 Entry 1003, National Archives II, College Park, Md.

the Five Year Plans were launched,[3] with their overriding, unrelenting emphasis on expansion of heavy industry. From that time, the Soviet consumer never had ceased to pay heavily to support that expansion.

The analysis of official price and earning data, presented in the table [below], indicates that the average Soviet worker would have to work about 45 percent longer in 1953 than he actually did in 1928 in order to buy the same weekly supply of seven essential foods (bread, potatoes, beef, butter, eggs, milk, and sugar). In particular, the Soviet worker, in effect, now has to work 67 percent longer to buy a pound of bread, about 43 percent longer to buy a pound of beef, and about 244 percent longer to buy a quart of milk. Potatoes, alone, because of the 50 percent price cut in 1953, are slightly cheaper than they were in 1928. Official Soviet data are not available for making the same sort of comparison for other consumer goods, particularly for clothing and footwear. All evidence, however, clearly indicates that clothing and footwear prices also have risen from 1928 to 1953 at a higher rate than money earnings.

In view of the fact that Moscow prices were used to represent the national average and that the 1953 earnings were estimated, the per-

Approximate Worktime Required to Buy Selected Foods at State-Fixed Prices in Moscow, April 1, 1928, and April 1, 1953

				APPROXIMATE WORKTIME		
	PRICE (IN RUBLES)		QUANTITY CONSUMED PER WEEK BY	IN HOURS		1953 AS PERCENT OF 1928
FOOD	1928	1953	4-PERSON FAMILY	1928	1953	
Rye Bread, 1 kg.	.080	1.35	9.84 kg.	2.71	4.52	167
Potatoes, 1 kg.	.085	.75	12.16 kg.	3.56	3.10	87
Beef, 1 kg.	.870	12.60	3.68 kg.	11.04	15.77	143
Butter, 1 kg.	2.430	26.75	.44 kg.	3.69	4.00	108
Sugar, 1 kg.	.620	9.09	1.80 kg.	3.85	5.57	145
Milk, 1 liter	.063	2.20	4.96 liter	1.08	3.71	344
Eggs, per 10	.200	6.88	6.40 units	.44	1.50	341
ALL 7 FOODS				26.37	38.17	145

[3] From 1928 to the dissolution of the USSR in 1991, government-dictated economic plans set targets for industrial, agricultural, and consumer goods production, usually pegged to a period of five years. The reference here is to Joseph Stalin's economic plans of the late 1920s and 1930s, intended to rapidly industrialize the nation's economy.

centage differences given are not to be considered as rigorously exact, but rather as approximations of the extent that real earnings in 1928 were higher than in 1953.

The increased worktime required to purchase the food consumed weekly by the average family of four persons presumedly answers the question why an exceptionally high percentage of Soviet women have to work outside the home in 1953. A Soviet worker, as sole supporter of a family of four, has to work over 75 percent of his time to buy only the seven foods in the same quantities which the average Moscow wage-earner family purchased in 1928. These seven items do not include various customary and particularly important foods in the Soviet worker's diet, such as cabbage and tea.

The price cut which went into effect in the U.S.S.R. on April 1, 1953, attracted an unusual amount of public attention as the first broad economic measure adapted under the Malenkov regime.[4] The cut was the sixth major one in the postwar period; it occurred at the same time of the year as most of the previous cuts and it gave the consumer fewer benefits than the first three cuts in the series. Yet the new Government seems to have made an effort to impress the Soviet public favorably by almost tripling the number of commodities covered in the 1952 decree and by increasing the size of the price cut for certain important foods. . . .

Observations of visitors to Moscow and reports in the Soviet press indicate that, while past Soviet price cuts have brought some saving to consumers, Soviet stores frequently are stocked inadequately with goods, both as to quantity and variety in styles and sizes.

The 1953 price cut, as those in previous years, assumedly will result in more sales to consumers. According to the annual report for 1952 of the Central Statistical Administration of the Council of U.S.S.R. Ministers, 10 percent more consumer goods were sold in 1952 than in 1951. Previous annual reports had claimed larger increases. Soviet figures indicate that consumer goods production continues to be secondary to the expansion of heavy industry or capital goods production. Available Soviet data show that during the period 1937–1952 capital goods production quadrupled while consumer goods production only doubled. Under the 1951–1955 Five Year Plan, capital goods production is scheduled to rise 13 percent annually and consumer goods, 11 percent.

Price cuts were stated by the Communist Party daily newspaper, *Pravda*, on April 3, 1953, to be the Party's and the Government's "most

---

[4] Georgy Malenkov served as Soviet premier from 1953 to 1955.

important means of raising the real earnings" of workers and farmers. This idea is in line with established Soviet policy in recent years not to raise wage rates. Reliable Soviet wage data are scarce and estimates vary as to average nominal earnings. While it is generally conceded that money earnings have risen since the mid-1920's, the rise in money earnings, taking the period as a whole, has not resulted in a higher level of living. On the contrary, during most of the prewar period and during World War II itself, consumer prices rose much faster than earnings. This already has been illustrated by the comparison of purchasing power of worktime in 1928 and 1953. The 1940 level of living was regained—according to an analysis of the United Nations Economic Commission for Europe—by 1950; however, this level itself was far below that of 1928.

The Soviet press made the usual claims that the 1953 price-cutting decree attested to the growing economic strength of the Soviet Union and to the rising level of living, and that, in contrast, the ordinary worker in the capitalist world, including the United States, was more and more "underfed and poverty-stricken." The figures refute these claims. They show that the average Moscow worker has to work twice as long for a pound of bread as a New York City worker. For potatoes, he has to work about three times as long; for beef, five times; for milk, six times; for eggs, seven times; for butter, nine times; and for tea, 21 times as long. Clothing, as indicated by the worktime required—about 10 to 20 times more in Moscow than in New York City—is very expensive to the average Soviet workers, whose monthly earnings have been estimated to be about 600 rubles. The absence of a price cut on woolen clothing—and men's clothing, in general—since 1950 indicates their scarcity.

23

NIKITA KHRUSHCHEV

Speech on the 1959 Soviet Seven-Year Economic Plan

January 1959

The Soviet Union's economy grew rapidly in the 1950s, fueling rising expectations for average citizens. In January 1959, Soviet Premier Nikita Khrushchev announced the Kremlin's official endorsement of a remarkably ambitious seven-year economic plan intended to boost agricultural productivity and spur production of consumer goods. The goals Khrushchev presented set the stage for his confidence at the Kitchen Debate six months later, reflecting his sincere belief that the Soviet Union was transitioning from an economy of sacrifice to one of abundance.

The 21st Congress of the Communist Party of the Soviet Union has convened to consider the control figures for development of the U.S.S.R. national economy in 1959–1965. Our Congress will discuss the program of further communist construction in the Soviet Union, of a new upswing in the economy, culture and the people's living standard. It is a great program. History has nothing to equal it in magnitude. In view of the tremendous importance of the seven-year plan of economic development, the September (1958) plenary session of the Central Committee found it necessary to convene the extraordinary Congress of our party to discuss the plan....

II. PRINCIPAL TASKS OF THE SEVEN-YEAR PLAN OF U.S.S.R. ECONOMIC DEVELOPMENT.—Comrades! Under the leadership of the Party, the Soviet people have reached such heights and have accomplished such vast changes in all spheres of economic, public and political life that our country now has the opportunity of entering a new and most important period of its development—the period of extensive building of communist society.

From Nikita Khrushchev, "On Control Figures for Development of the U.S.S.R. National Economy in 1959–1965," *Pravda*, January 28, 1959. Translated in *Current Digest of the Soviet Press* 11, no. 2: 13–19.

The principal tasks of this period are to establish the material and technical base for communism, to strengthen further the economic and defensive might of the U.S.S.R. and simultaneously to provide ever fuller satisfaction of the growing material and spiritual requirements of the people. The historic task of overtaking and surpassing the most highly developed of the capitalist countries in per capita output must be accomplished. . . .

In speaking of the perspectives for development of basic industries and electrification of the national economy, one must dwell on machine building, which will continue to develop at a rapid pace.

The seven-year plan provides for accelerated development of all modern branches of machine building, particularly heavy machine building, instrument manufacture and the production of automatic and electronic devices. Special attention is being devoted to the designing and production of the latest machinery, utilizing the achievements and discoveries of science and technology, particularly radioelectronics, semiconductors, ultrasonics and radioactive isotopes.

More than 50 powerful, high-efficiency rolling mills, with wide application of the principles of continuous rolling and automation, will be built for the iron and steel industry and put in operation. One of the first-priority tasks is to develop a wide range of the latest chemical equipment. . . .

The high level of development of heavy industry and accomplishment of the measures for an advance in agriculture will make it possible to increase considerably the output of foodstuffs and consumer goods.

In the course of the seven years, gross output of light industry is to rise approximately 50% and of the food industry 70%. Production of cotton fabrics will increase 33% to 38%, woolen fabrics 65%, silks 76%, leather footwear 45%, meat 110%, butter 58%, dairy products 120%, sugar 76% to 90%, and fish 60%.

In addition to increasing output, light industry now confronts as a foremost task the achievement of a considerable improvement in the range and quality of output. Consumer goods must be of high quality, attractive, handsomely packed, and packaged. To meet the goals for increasing output and improving quality of consumer goods and foodstuffs it is planned to build more than 1600 new enterprises for light industry and the food industry. In addition, a large number of existing enterprises will be reconstructed. . . .

Along with the great development of light industry, it is planned in the seven years to double the output of household goods and domestic chore-lightening machines and appliances produced at machine-building and woodworking plants and the consumer goods shops of other factories. . . .

A further mighty advance in socialist agriculture will be of tremendous importance to building communism and raising the people's living standard.

As defined by the decision of the December plenary session of the Central Committee, the basic task in agriculture in the next seven years is to reach a level of production which will enable us to satisfy fully the food requirements of the public and the raw-material needs of industry and to meet all of the state's other needs for agricultural products.

A 70% rise in the gross output of agriculture is envisaged for 1959–1965. The average annual increase in output will amount to 8%. It may be noted that the average annual growth in agricultural output in the United States in the past seven years has been less than 2%. . . .

For the next few years the main line in crop farming will continue to be the utmost expansion of grain production as the basis of all agricultural production. In recent years the grain output has been increased chiefly by extending the sown area. We shall continue to develop new lands, but on a smaller scale than hitherto; this will not bring a large increase in the gross grain yield, since considerable areas will be sown to industrial crops or will lie fallow.

Now that the collective and state farms[1] possess qualified personnel and modern machinery and are in a position to perform farm operations fast and well, to use more organic and mineral fertilizer and to sow select seed, there is every requisite for increasing the yield of grain crops by an average of three to four centners per hectare throughout the country in the immediate future and thereby fulfilling and overfulfilling the control figures for the gross grain crop.

In animal husbandry the chief task in the next seven years is to increase the production of meat, milk, wool and eggs. This should be accomplished through a sharp rise in the number of all kinds of livestock, poultry and rabbits at the collective and state farms and by raising the meat and milk yields.

---

[1] State farms, or *sovkhozy*, were distinguished from *kolkhozy* (collective farms) by the fact that they were formally owned by the state rather than by a collective. After World War II, Soviet agricultural policymakers pushed to convert many collective farms to state farms, seeing them as a higher form of socialist development. Workers on state farms generally received better and more reliable pay for their work than did collective farmers, but their freedoms—such as the ability to move within the Soviet Union—were strictly constrained.

The fodder base must be strengthened even more persistently, chiefly by raising more corn, potatoes and sugar beet and by growing protein feeds such as clover, alfalfa, vetch-oats mixtures, peas, lupine and other crops, depending on the features of the individual zone. Serious interest must be shown in growing soy beans, which are very valuable as a food, technical and fodder crop.

Our country has advanced to first place in the world in total output of milk and butter. Within the next few years we shall not only overtake but considerably surpass the United States in per capita output of these items. At the same time, much work will have to be done to put all potentialities and opportunities to use to increase meat production by 2.5 to three times, to surpass the seven-year plan goal and to implement the appeal of the country's leading collective and state farms to overtake the United States in per capita output of livestock products.

These high rates of growth in agricultural output are based on the tremendous advantages of the socialist economic system and the increased might of our industry, which is supplying all the necessary equipment and machinery for large-scale, mechanized farming.

In the seven years, agriculture is to be provided with more than 1,000,000 tractors, approximately 400,000 grain combines, a large number of other machines and a great deal of equipment. Electrical equipment used by the collective and state farms will almost double.

Electrification of all collective farms will be completed in the main by the end of the seven years, while electrification of the state farms will be completed considerably earlier. Electric power consumption in the countryside will almost quadruple, and this will make it possible to reduce farm production costs by more than 19,000,000,000,000 rubles and to take another stride forward in further developing the culture and improving the life of the collective-farm villages. . . .

Our enemies abroad cry that the Soviet seven-year plan was drawn up with emphasis on development of heavy industry and will demand "sacrifices" on the part of the public. Our plan does indeed envisage large capital investment in developing heavy industry. But could it be otherwise?

To have a sufficiency of consumer goods means of production are required, metal must be obtained, machines built, automatic machine lines installed to work for man and to satisfy his requirements. Even to grow such a simple product as potatoes, a metal share for the wooden plow was needed in the past. But we are advancing toward communist society, we want machines to do all the main jobs, with man merely directing them. Formerly each peasant used to skimp and save when he wanted to buy a horse. He well knew that if he had a horse he could farm, but without a horse he would starve. Times have changed. Development of industry, growth of the means of production—this is our powerful steed. If we have the steed we shall have everything else as well. (*Applause.*)

During the early five-year plans,[2] when the question was one of life or death for the Soviet land—the world's only socialist country, encircled by capitalist countries—the Soviet people strained every muscle and consciously made sacrifices to break the grip of age-old backwardness and establish a powerful socialist economy. But even at that time the Party and the state did everything possible to improve the people's material situation. Today we have a different level of development, other possibilities, other forces, and we firmly set the task of considerably improving the well-being of the Soviet people. Hence no one can talk of "sacrifices" without distorting the truth.

Let the "critics" of our plan try to name a single capitalist government that would chart so great an increase in popular consumption as we have planned! Let them name a bourgeois state in which a reduction of the working day has been scheduled with the same and even higher wages. The working class and the working people of the capitalist countries have to wage a bitter struggle for this against the exploiters. The capitalist world does not and cannot have governments and states with such concern for the working people. (*Applause.*) . . .

In the West they say that we have issued a "challenge." Well, if they like the word, let us consider that we have. But it is a challenge to compete in peaceful economic development and in raising the people's living standard. . . .

We want to compete not in the arms race and the production of atomic and hydrogen bombs and missiles, but in the production of manufactured goods, meat, butter, milk, clothing, footwear and other consumer goods.

Let the people judge for themselves which system best satisfies their requirements and let them judge each system duly!

---

[2] Joseph Stalin introduced the First Five-Year Plan in 1928, replacing Lenin's New Economic Policy. Stalin intended the plan to begin making the Soviet Union economically self-sufficient, primarily through massive investments in industrial production.

24

V. YE. SEMICHASTNY

Speech on Communist Youth and Consumerism

January 1959

Soviets, like Americans, often held ambivalent views about consumerism. In January and February 1959, a special meeting of the Congress of the Communist Party—the supreme ruling body of the Soviet Communist Party—was held to discuss the 1959 seven-year economic plan. In this speech before the assembled party dignitaries, an official in the youth division of the Communist Party expressed reservations about the plan, suggesting that too much emphasis on private consumption contradicted communist ideology.

Through Young Communist League channels more than 5,000,000 young people have responded in a short time to public appeals to go to the virgin lands and construction projects of the East, the North and Siberia, to participate in harvesting the new lands and to take jobs in animal husbandry.[1] Is this not evidence of the mass heroism of our young people, their spirit of sacrifice, their boundless love for the motherland and their devotion to the cause of the Party? (*Applause.*) This is how it has been, this is how it is, and we assure the Party Congress that this is how it always will be: The Young Communist League, loyal aide of the Communist Party, will execute any assignment the Party gives it!

While reporting to the Congress on the achievements of the Y.C.L., we recognize that there are still serious shortcomings in the work of the Y.C.L. organizations. Many of the organizations, while conducting mass campaigns in a general way, often fail to reach each young individual

---

[1] The Young Communist League, or *Komsomol*, was charged with recruiting young Soviets from the more populated western regions of the USSR to work the new farms of the Virgin Lands Campaign (see Introduction). Ordinary members of the Young Communist League ranged in age from fourteen to twenty-eight, but administrators—such as V. Ye. Semichastny—could be older.

From a speech by Comrade V. Ye. Semichastny, Young Communist League Central Committee, *Pravda*, January 30, 1959. Translated in *Current Digest of the Soviet Press* 11, nos. 6–7: 4–5.

and still have many failures and shortcomings in the work of political education. To our great regret, there are still instances of drunkenness and hooliganism among young people. . . .

Comrades! As we enter the path of extensive construction of communism the Party points out that questions of communist education of the working people, especially of the young generation, must become central in all the work of public organizations. . . .

How are we to form a fully developed individual? How should the communist attitude toward work be instilled in young people? Life itself, of course, answers these and many similar questions for young people. But it is to be wished that the theory and practice of communist upbringing of young people, especially problems of communist morality, received more attention from the social scientists, especially from our philosophers, and that one could read about them in the magazines and in books.

Comrades! Everybody knows what great concern our party shows for raising the cultural level of the working people. A big new step will be taken in this direction in the forthcoming seven years. Instilling high culture is an essential part of the communist upbringing of young people. We must show young people the world of beauty, teach them to understand the arts, painting, music, and protect them from hack work, vulgarity and trash. It is very good that adult universities of culture and various clubs for the pursuit of special interests have already appeared in some cities. Our writers, composers and artists have taken the first steps toward close contact with the communist labor brigades. Unfortunately, we are devoting insufficient attention to the esthetic education of young people. That is why vulgarity and hack work find too much scope here and there. I shall cite the following instances.

Inferior and inartistic goods are often sold at markets and railroad stations in many cities, including province and even republic centers. Blue-violet stuffed animals that have an extremely faint resemblance to cats and dogs, paper doilies with fat swans and by no means ethereal mermaids, horrible "golden" little statuettes—all this unfortunately moves into the homes of our people, including young people. This is not because Soviet people have bad taste. It is mainly because we offer little by way of contrast to this hack work. Wide reproduction of the best paintings of Russian and Soviet artists must be set on a solid basis and conditions created for the further development of traditional crafts and folk art. . . .

Communist society is a society of collectivists. Therefore, we must give people from the years of childhood the feeling of unity of personal and social interests, the team spirit and readiness for mutual help. Unfortunately, we still pay little attention to these questions. May this not be the reason why some of our young people still display egotism, individualism and other survivals of private-property psychology and morality? We say to a child from the first days: This is your toy, your book, your bicycle. Later, when he becomes an adult, he says: This is my car, my summer cottage, my motorcycle. (*Laughter.*) I think that we should now introduce the wonderful word "our" more widely into the practice of communist-collective living. This is a great problem.

Let us take the question of rental centers. Why should we not open such centers literally everywhere so that whoever desires may rent for a small fee a bicycle, a car, a motorcycle, a motor boat or similar things? Our public organizations could take care of this as well. I think that we should think seriously about this.

One more matter of everyday life. Stores, repair and service combines, dressmaking shops and laundries—they all function as a rule, at hours when most of the working people are at work. People are obliged to spend their free day shopping, wasting their time. In our opinion it is advisable to consider whether stores and shops should not work longer hours on weekday evenings and be closed on days off. The free day should be used as it is intended, for sports, theaters, clubs and motion pictures. This will also help in the education of young people.

All the thoughts and hopes of our people are with the Party. There is not a single Y.C.L. heart that does not beat in unison with the heart of the Party, that is not consumed with flaming love for the Party and that does not stretch out toward the Party, as everything that lives stretches out toward the sun, the source of life.

Soviet young men and women love the Communist Party more than life itself because in it lies our strength and steadfastness. It is our teacher and inspired builder, it is our educator and leader.

25

A Soviet Woman Questions Consumerism
1962

In December 1961, a Russian newspaper for the youth division of the Communist Party, Komsomolskaya Pravda *("Young Communist League Truth"), published a questionnaire soliciting readers' "ideas about the young family." The newspaper published many of the more than three thousand responses it received, among them the following response from a self-described "housewife."*

I cannot talk about family life, because mine was a marriage of convenience. . . . If it were possible to see even two months ahead into the future, many young girls would think twice before marrying for any other consideration except love. I say this on the basis of personal experience. Eleven years ago I married a man 20 years my senior because he had plenty of money and a highly paid job. Today I have everything—a TV set, a refrigerator, a radio, a vacuum cleaner, a washing machine, a Volga car—but not love; and all these material comforts about which so many other people dream merely weigh me down, throttle me, don't let me breathe. My relationship with my husband is very bad. But we have a son who loves his father, and for his sake I must suffer in silence. I want to warn young people—a marriage of convenience is a terrible marriage.

T. SH.
At this point a housewife, 30 years old. Lvov Region.

From "Youth Has Its Say on Love and Marriage," *Soviet Review* (August 1962): 21–40.

3

An Easier Life for Our Housewives

The American National Exhibition in Moscow showcased much more than televisions, appliances, and automobiles. American women were also on prominent display. Fashion models donned bathing suits and country-club dance attire, a beauty salon featured the newest cosmetics, and home economists in cleanly tailored dresses welcomed visitors to the model kitchens (see Documents 9 and 10). These women embodied the stylish domesticity of the 1950s that fueled American consumer society and glamorized the kitchen, the command center of the private home. Laborsaving devices and convenience foods enabled middle-class housewives to take over work previously performed by hired help, while postwar prosperity expanded the ranks of those who aspired to middle-class status and its chief signifiers: a male "breadwinner" and a stay-at-home wife who managed the household, cared for children, and prepared family meals. Nixon conjured up this entire package of domestic aspirations when he explained to Khrushchev that "what we want to do is make easier the life of our housewives" (see Document 5).

The celebration of homemaking, however, often concealed the more far-reaching social change of postwar America: the increasing number of white married women with children who entered the U.S. workforce. While working wives and mothers may not have directly challenged traditional assumptions about women's roles in the 1950s, their paychecks helped to underwrite family purchasing patterns, and their existence was certainly recognized by peddlers of both advice and consumer goods. The era's domestic ideology also papered over another obvious fact: Not all housework was pleasant or fulfilling. The cultural and social strains resulting from these cross-cutting pressures inevitably found their way to the kitchen, where food preparation became a focal point of debate over women's self-definition as housewives and cooks.

Socialist critics had long disparaged what they viewed, in Khrushchev's words, as "the capitalist attitude toward women" (see Document 5). They argued that capitalist systems confined women to the home, fetishized family over society, and prevented women's full absorption into the public sphere of productive labor. Indeed, women's issues received a great deal of government attention during the Khrushchev era: Officials openly acknowledged women's "triple burden" of paid work, parenting, and household duties, and they made highly publicized promises for more public services, such as nurseries and children's day care, to lighten women's loads. But because Soviet commentators and political leaders like Khrushchev never revised their assumptions about women's ultimate responsibility for household management, they also embraced the liberating potential of the modern kitchen—its efficient layout and technological wizardry—as warmly as any American politician or corporate executive. Representatives of the two superpowers may not have agreed on the ideological reasons to free their housewives from drudgery, but they appeared to share a common vision that household technology was both liberating and necessary.

A Servantless Kitchen?

26

LITA PRICE AND HARRIET BONNET

How to Manage without a Maid

1942

Middle-class American families had long employed domestic servants to lighten the housewife's burden and to enable her to manage and beautify the home. While the number of available servants had begun to decrease in the two decades before World War II, the war accelerated the process as working-class women — many of them African American — left domestic service for higher-paying factory and defense jobs. How to Manage without a Maid *offered advice to homemakers caught off guard by the decline in household help.*

From Lita Price and Harriet Bonnet, *How to Manage without a Maid* (New York: Bobbs-Merrill, 1942), 26–29, 74–77, 187–88, 193–95.

Who Wants to Come Out of the Kitchen?

Maid service is getting harder and harder to find at any price and only too often, even if you pay top wages, you will have to put up with help which is unskilled, unwilling and seldom permanent. Usually as soon as a house worker can find another type of employment, she will leave you flat and you have still another maid to break in. Unskilled maids require a great deal of supervision, and in the beginning require almost as much of your time as you would spend doing the work yourself—if you have a modern, well-equipped kitchen. And have you ever counted up what having any maid costs you in dollars and cents?

Of course, wages differ in different parts of the country but seldom can you obtain an even halfway satisfactory maid for less than seven dollars a week. . . .

Maybe a maid is worth all this to you and more—a good permanent one certainly is, if you can afford her—but all over America servants are becoming so inefficient, temporary, arrogant or expensive, and often so difficult to procure at all, that many women now prefer doing their own work. It may have been true in Grandmother's day, that two black hands were the greatest labor-saving device for doing housework, but the same does not hold true now when there is so much electrical and mechanical equipment on the market. . . .

Few housewives who have always had maids have made a thorough study of what really constitutes a modern, up-to-date kitchen. We can't blame any of you who haven't, because most of the help you have had would not have understood the use of these new mechanical time-savers. Furthermore, they would not have taken the proper care of them to insure their efficiency. But if you yourself are going to do the housework and cooking, it's a different story. You may feel you'd like to invest the amount of one year's maid wages in lightening your own work, or making your working conditions more attractive.

Electric kitchens are the triumph of this machine age. One nationally known company even advertises: "A new combination, fully equipped kitchen-and-dining-lounge with service bar and indirect lighting in changeable colors. . . . It converts the kitchen into a new guest room." We've never seen one of these marvels and few of us choose to spend so much in our kitchens, but you may be interested in knowing just what decorative heights the kitchen has attained!

But to come down to earth, if you're going to do your own work, you'll start and finish the working day in the kitchen because all families have to eat. First then, in planning to make your kitchen more convenient, think about floor space. If you live in a rented house or apartment, there is seldom anything you can do about this, unless by rearranging your refrigerator or stove so as to be more convenient to the sink, you can seemingly create more room. However, you may be going to build a new home or you may be remodeling; then whatever you do, plan first.

Ask yourself what will go on in your kitchen. Cooking? Of course! Cleaning? Naturally! Do you entertain much? Do you have adequate serving space for parties? Are the children under foot? Could you arrange for a play pen? Or could you cut off a small corner with a folding fence? Do you need a telephone in the kitchen? Or a desk? Is your laundry work done in the kitchen? Can you make room for a washing machine, or ironer or ironing board? How can you group them in a unit? Do you sew there? Can you make that more convenient? Or perhaps you use one end of the kitchen, or would like to, for a breakfast nook? Can you arrange a place for a comfortable chair? Can you afford a ventilating fan? Do you need more windows for light and air? All these matters should be taken into consideration as you plan to build, remodel or rearrange. . . .

Three a Day (and Sometimes Tea Makes Four)

When you first start to do your own work, it may seem as if mealtime is perpetually coming up. You have to hop out of bed every morning to get breakfast; stop doing something seemingly important to get lunch; and rush home from social engagements to get dinner. You don't mind the housework, for that can be dovetailed into your other interests and activities, but the regularity of having to get meals on the table *three times* every day and clean up after each one is often irritating beyond words, until you *learn a few tricks* about the *art of cooking and serving*.

DRAMATIZE YOUR MEALS

If you have a flare for the dramatic, there's no better place to use your talent than in planning and serving meals. An exotic decorative touch here and there will transfer the most commonplace menu into a festive one, besides giving you the thrill of having expressed your personality. Make an occasion of everyday dinners by using colorful pottery, candlelight, unusual centerpieces (fruit or figurines will be just as effective as flowers), or by decorating your platters of food. We guarantee this [is] a sure cure for any irritation you may have felt in the past about having to cook.

If your family is large, the buffet style of service makes an exciting variation to the humdrum of everyday service. Just put the food on large platters and dishes on the buffet or the dining-room table, give each person an individual tray and let him walk around to help himself cafeteria style. If the family is small, you might serve the individual plates in the kitchen, instead of at the dining table. It may be more formal to serve plates at the table but any departure from the customary service will often make a meal seem more appealing. If you have small children, it is sometimes more practical to feed them in the kitchen or breakfast nook before your family dinner so that the adult members can enjoy their meal in peace. And if you have babies, we've found it's far simpler to train them to play in pens in another room or to stay in their beds, rather than allow them to sit in a high chair at the table and disrupt the family meals.

Make your table service *elegantly simple*, whatever style you decide upon. Too much folderol will not only wear you out but it's bad taste. It's like wearing your velvet evening dress with saddle oxfords. The two just don't go together. So, except when the boss comes to dinner or you are entertaining formally, restrain yourself; save your most elaborate accessories and dine simply. You've no idea how much more satisfactory as a steady diet this will be, and how much more energy you'll have left over for fun.

But this does not mean you should live on "boiled dinners," though they *are* good on occasion. Rather put lots of variety, even drama, into your menus. It's an easy matter to open up cans or use frozen foods with a simple sauce; serve cold cuts or chop suey or barbecue brought home from the delicatessen; or use packaged and semi-prepared foods. But in rotation you should also feature a favorite main dish or dessert of each member of your family. If your husband speaks feelingly of the beauty and aroma of standing roast, it's up to you occasionally to provide one even if it does take time to cook. If your son likes biscuits, why not have them often? You can always buy them canned, all ready to pop into the oven, if you don't want to take time to make them.

These two whims should give you ideas. Families often get tired of too much semi-prepared food, but if you include one good "home-cooked" dish which will go with packaged or canned foods, you'll acquire the reputation of being a marvelous cook and manager.

By planning ahead, you can arrange to have meals at odd hours to suit the family needs. One of the main disadvantages of having a cook is that usually meals have to be on schedule. That's as it should be, of course, for a maid should be able to count on getting away from her job at a definite time, but when you're the cook, your time is your own. If you are playing bridge in the afternoon, who cares if you have a late dinner? No one will, if you aren't cross in your turn when the children are late getting home from skating or your husband from the office. In order to be able to manage these situations without any great inconvenience to yourself and still set an appetizing table, we believe the only way is to do all the preliminary jobs long before mealtime. Then by spending a minimum amount of time in the kitchen shortly before the family is ready to eat, you can seemingly whip up a marvelous meal on the spur of the moment. . . .

Double Duty

There may arise in any woman's life occasions or even lengthy periods of time when housekeeping is the least important part of her life. Specifically, we refer to those women who have double duties which demand not only an efficient household but also certain definite responsibilities apart from routine housekeeping. . . .

The career woman who has to spend eight hours a day taking orders from a far-from-silent boss or the woman who has her own business which makes constant demands on her time and thought has little energy or desire to go into intricate matters of housekeeping. Out of necessity she has to minimize all domestic work, and after all, this can be made easy if she takes advantage of modern scientific help. . . .

Having outside help come once or twice a week to clean, do light laundry, prepare dinner and possibly to mend is a boon to any Career Woman's career and we believe she justly deserves it. But when such a thing is impossible, she must try to keep herself living on her schedule and in good health and spirits.

There is not such a thing as an average business woman-housekeeper. One is unmarried and living alone, one is sharing an apartment with another bachelor girl, another has a small child whom she has to take to a nursery school before she goes to work or an older child who helps out with jobs at home. Another woman keeps house for herself and husband only, while both work. Where there are two or more people living together, no one of whom is at home or at leisure during the day, the actual responsibility of cooking, marketing, dishwashing and cleaning should be shared equally. Such an arrangement often works out to the advantage of everybody, especially when it is worked on a plan for each person.

A modern husband is generally co-operative, if the wife makes out schedules and allots jobs to them both. Quite often, however, men, more than women, have great aversions to certain jobs which they consider "sissy." For example, we know a husband who will do, cheerfully, all menial jobs, such as dishwashing and garbage emptying, but positively can't bear bedmaking. Hence it's a wise wife who takes into consideration her husband's likes and dislikes and allots to herself the jobs he doesn't want to do. Many men pride themselves on their cookery and if a woman is smart enough to capitalize on this fact, she can make her kitchen a rendezvous for the male gourmets of her acquaintance and add much social life to her home.

27

Goodbye Mammy, Hello Mom

March 1947

Before World War II, more than 85 percent of all wage-earning African American women worked as domestic servants. During the war, the total number of black women working as domestics dropped by half. This abrupt change elicited the sort of racist commentary evident in the previous document, but it also allowed African Americans to imagine the postwar era on their own terms. Ebony, *launched in 1945, was an illustrated monthly magazine marketed to upwardly mobile blacks. This editorial captured the combination of expectation and anxiety that shaped African Americans' responses to the era's domestic ideology.*

Something startling and significant has been happening in the kitchens—and kitchenettes, too—of Negro families during the past five years. It has not made headlines in the Negro press but certainly stacks up with the biggest news of the past decade.

Just ask Junior, who's been getting his bread and peanut butter sandwiches regularly after school and finding that rip in his blue jeans mended when he goes out to play. Or ask Pop, who now comes home to a hot supper of pork chops and greens instead of eating a lukewarm blue plate dinner at Nick's Café or Sadie's Tea Shoppe. And Sister Kate

---

From "Goodbye Mammy, Hello Mom," editorial, *Ebony*, March 1947, 36.

will join in spreading the glad tidings too, because now she goes to the movies with friend Johnnie instead of baby-sitting with Junior.

Yes, it seems Mom has come home.

No one knows just when Mom came home. It was some time around Pearl Harbor Day, just a little after Pop went out and got a war job that put the family on a balanced budget for the first time in years. Right off, he told Mom to tell "Madam" that her maid was through. But Mom said "No." It was too sudden. She hung on for a while until her next-door neighbor told her about war jobs for women. That's when Mom dropped her dust pan and dish rag and got herself a welding outfit.

Before long, there was money in the bank. And Pop even became an investor: he had more than $500 worth of war bonds.

It was too good to last. But when reconversion and the layoffs came, Papa was able to get another job—even if the pay wasn't as high. And Mom—well, she decided she would go home.

Negro Mothers Come Home

And so today in thousands of Negro homes, the Negro mother has come home—come home perhaps for the first time since 1619 when the first Negro families landed at Jamestown, Virginia.

In those early days, the Negro mother was a slave, working the fields from sunup to sundown. She was a breeder of more slaves, considered no better nor worse than a brood mare. Slaves were mated to get more human work animals; then families were broken up on the slave block. Husband and wife were shipped to different plantations to start the breeding process all over again.

But somewhere in those dark days, it was discovered that beneath a black as well as a white skin there beat the heart of a mother filled with love of children. And so the slavers, who had not hesitated to prostitute the bodies of Negro womanhood, did the same to the souls of Negro mothers.

That's how Mammy was born.

Mammy was such a devoted and loyal mother that she soon became celebrated in song and literature. And when slavery perished on the parapets of Appomattox and Gettysburg, Mammy didn't die. For more than a half-century, she hung on as a Dixie institution, paid perhaps $10 a month and an occasional pot of black eyed peas or an old dress.

It finally took modern industrial life to inter Mammy. But in her place came the domestic, forced out of her home to supplement the low wages, if any, of her husband. Paltry as were her earnings from housework, they still meant something. Less than 10 per cent of the working mothers added more than $20 a week to family income, as a Harlem study showed, but that little bit extra was in many instances the difference between starvation and two or three meals a day.

Kitchen Revolution

Then World War II caused a kitchen revolution.

It took Negro mothers out of white kitchens, put them in factories and shipyards. When it was all over, they went back to kitchens—but this time their own.

During the war, Negro husbands were for the first time in many years earning enough to support their families without supplemental income from their wives. As Negro men dropped their brooms and mops to move out of menial occupations into industry, their wives were able to stay at home and become housewives.

There have been no "Welcome Home" signs hung up on the door, though well there might have been, but the Negro mother is finding a warm greeting from her family. The cooking over which the white folks used to go into ecstasies is now reserved for her own family and they really appreciate it. And Junior doesn't spend as much time in the street with "the gang": he's putting more time into his homework. Domestic peace seems to be the order of things since she came home.

She Can't Live on Love

The million Negro women who were counted in domestic service before 1941 have dwindled away until today the law of supply and demand has sent the wages of domestics up 1,000 per cent in the last 11 years, according to the New York State Department of Labor. Back in 1935, the average weekly wage of New York domestic workers was $3.50. Today it is $30.

Some six out of ten Negro women in Manhattan still are employed as domestics in private homes, says the New York Urban League, but the figure is steadily going down as more and more Negro mothers go home—to stay. What's bothering many sociologists, however, is how long can the trend last? All that's needed to knock it flat, many maintain, is a whiff of depression.

Much as the Negro mother loves her home, she can't live on love. In the more than three million Negro households in the nation, the economic barometer seems to have its most drastic effects on the colored mother. She is the last resort, the ever-important reserve to hold the family together when unemployment strikes. Statistics show that as Negro industrial employment drops, the proportion of working Negro married women goes up and it can be expected to happen again . . . if and when.

A Woman's Place

Whether you politely and optimistically call it a "slight recession" or a "big depression," nobody denies that the time *is* coming, especially for colored families, when Mom will have to earn some money again. But even if she is forced back into white kitchens, the Negro mother—once having tasted freedom and independence in her own home—will not stay. She is bound to escape the first chance she gets.

Many of the country's Moms are spending a little time on the headlines these days and learning where they stand in relation to the world around them. They are learning that they need not go back to being Mrs. Palmer's Honey.

Perhaps single girls in domestic service today hold the key to the future for many Negro mothers who may once again have to leave their homes and doorkeys around their children's necks when they go to work. Now when cooks and houseworkers are scarce and sought-after, labor unions of domestics are getting their start. Tomorrow, with domestics all-too-available, may be too late.

Not that a woman's place is in the kitchen necessarily. Nobody wants to tie a woman to her hearthstone with hackneyed phrases and ideas about where her place is. But every family should be able to live on the income of one breadwinner. And every woman should be able to choose whether she wants to devote her days to her children and her home or to a career girl's job.

Perhaps in not too many months, Mom will have no choice.

But it doesn't have to be that way always. Not if Mom gets wise.

28

JEAN HARRIS

You Have 1001 Servants in Your Kitchen

March 1951

House Beautiful, *founded in 1896, is the longest-running interior design magazine in the United States. While only the most affluent Americans could afford the high-end architectural and decorative styles it featured in the 1950s, many middle-class women eagerly emulated the modern, streamlined taste in home design that the magazine promoted. In 1951,* House Beautiful *introduced a new section called the "Daily Arts of Good Living" and asked its readers whether they had discovered "the new freedom in homemaking." It exhorted them to learn about new foods, techniques, and mechanical devices, because "eating well no longer means drudgery in the kitchen." This article was the first to appear in the new section.*

Not all of your kitchen is in your home. The thousands of people working in canneries, creameries, packing plants and frozen food plants are just as much your servants as if they were under your roof. For the hard, dirty exacting work of food preparation is done there by them. Only the easy part is left for you to do.

You may think servants have disappeared, because none are on your payroll. But you are mistaken. True, you don't have to look at them or listen to them. But they are still working for you, *if* you let them and know how to utilize the contribution they can make.

You pay for these thousands of servants when you buy mass-produced foods. But their services cost less, per manpower unit, than if they were on your payroll. Thanks to the advantages of mass production, your money can buy more services than you could obtain any other way. As many people are "waiting on you" as if you were the richest oriental potentate.

From Jean Harris, "You Have 1001 Servants in Your Kitchen," *House Beautiful*, March 1951, 74–77, 150.

But not all families are sharing in this new utopian situation. Prejudice about processed foods is keeping millions of women chained to old-fashioned, unnecessary drudgery. It has long been a conceit among women who take their homemaking seriously that using canned and processed foods is not the best way. It has been made a virtue to use only fresh foods, even though such foods may have been in transit for five to ten days. This conceit started, quite understandably, with our grandmothers and was perpetuated by our mothers. They had plenty of reason to be suspicious of the early experimental efforts of the food industry. Since cooking habits are handed down from mother to daughter, this prejudice has persisted, even though the causes are no longer valid.

This prejudice flourished for another reason; lack of understanding about how to cook to gourmet standards with processed foods.

When a woman, who is particular about quality, makes a tentative try at using a processed food, she is likely to serve it exactly as it comes out of the can or package. This proves to her, all over again, that she's been right all along. For the processed food will be underseasoned, or seasoned with things she doesn't like, or made by a recipe she doesn't approve of. And back she goes to preparing everything from scratch—her way.

What she doesn't know is that she *could* have found, from among the dozens of brands of one foodstuff, a type that *did* fit her needs. If she wanted to do her own seasoning, she could have found a brand that had almost no seasoning, but which still had the advantage of no handwork of peeling, slicing, stemming or whatever. That foodstuff would be a better product, basically, because it was processed at the exactly right moment of fruition. If she had located that just-right-for-her brand, she could have gone on to put the stamp of her own brand of cooking on it—but without the same consumption of time and energy. If she could get over that first hurdle (of knowing that processed foods must be used differently), then she could go on to harness the other thousands of food possibilities, and extend her cooking repertoire to exciting horizons. . . .

Nowhere has the dead hand of the past lain heavier than in the food field. The fact that canned foods were not very good 20 or 30 years ago, when our mothers and grandmothers first tried them, has set up a mental road-block about all processed goods ever since. Whenever you find a family that strives for fine eating, you also find a prejudice against processed food. . . .

But since most canned foods are still prepared for a very general cross-sectional taste, the trick of using them is to treat them like raw materials. Combine them, supplement their flavor, make them into the basis for something else. This opens a great field for good eating without much work. For instance, a really good main dish, made entirely of easy-to-get canned ingredients, is made with a can of cream of mushroom soup, a can of cream of tomato soup, a pound of crabmeat, a teaspoon of curry powder, and two to four tablespoons of sherry added after the dish is taken from the stove. It's as gourmet as anything, yet it can be put together in about ten minutes.

29

YOUNGSTOWN KITCHENS

Whether You Build, Buy or Modernize

1953

The following advertisement, produced by a company that manufactured steel cabinets, sold a vision of family togetherness along with an updated kitchen layout.

Youngstown Kitchens, "Whether You Build, Buy or Modernize," 1953.

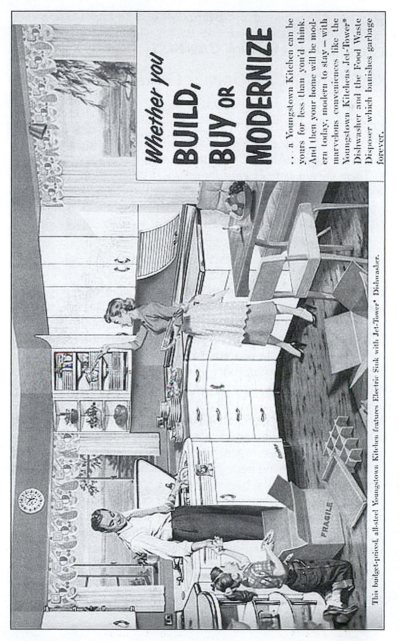

Figure 7. *A Youngstown Kitchen*

30

POPPY CANNON

The Can-Opener Cookbook

1952

Poppy Cannon began her career as a food journalist writing columns for
Mademoiselle *magazine, which targeted an audience of young working
women. There she honed her signature approach to "short-cut" cookery.
With the assistance of convenience products, she insisted, meals could be
prepared swiftly yet glamorously.* The Can-Opener Cookbook *was the
first of her many best-selling cookbooks published from the 1950s to the
1970s.*

Something new has been added to the age-old saga of good eating.
America, never before gastronomically renowned despite its wealth of
excellent ingredients, burgeoning larders, fertile farm lands, herds and
flocks, has developed epicurean interests—but with a difference. Our
cooking ideas and ideals have their roots in many lands and cultures,
but our new way of achieving gourmet food can only happen here—in
the land of the mix, the jar, the frozen-food package, and the ubiquitous
can opener.

At one time a badge of shame, hallmark of the lazy lady and the care-
less wife, today the can opener is fast becoming a magic wand, especially in the hands of those brave, young women, nine million of them
(give or take a few thousand here and there), who are engaged in frying
as well as bringing home the bacon.

There has developed among them a pride in preparing and serving
interesting meals. It is no longer considered chic, charming, or "intellectual" to be ignorant in the kitchen, but always there is the problem of
time, the crowding of many varied interests.

To the rescue comes the manufacturer of so-called ready-to-serve
foods. Actually, at least in gourmet terms, they are not *quite* ready to
serve, but they do provide the basis for any number of prideful, even

From Poppy Cannon, *The Can-Opener Cookbook* (New York: Crowell, 1952), 1–6.

complicated, specialties. The modern cook looks at it this way: other people have the responsibility for the selection of my raw materials, the cleaning and preliminary preparation. When I ply my busy little can opener I come onto the scene the way a chef comes in after a corps of kitchen helpers has done the scullery chores—the drudgery of cooking. Armed with a can opener I become the artist-cook, the master, the creative chef.

The use of a can opener may not be new, but the gourmet approach definitely is, for our new-style wielder of the can opener is a perfectionist. Gone are the days when anything quick was considered a triumph and concoctions of tuna fish, cream of mushroom soup, and potato chips flourished among the hurry-up menus. Now we are becoming classicists, and are analyzing the complicated, work-consuming recipes of olden days. We are discovering how the canned stews and chicken fricassees, canned gravy, soup, or consommé can be properly employed in today's living. . . .

Or, take the lowly meat ball—not wildly exciting, certainly, but there is inspiration to be found among the Hindus, where cookery is a sacred ceremony, a recipe for Kofta-Ka-Kari (Forcemeat Ball Curries). This is achieved simply by adding to the meat balls and their gravy, the best available curry powder, a well-crushed clove of garlic, dried parsley, thyme, marjoram, and rosemary. Heat and serve inside a ring of cooked rice, decorated prettily with french fried onions (another excellent canned specialty) and pass the chutney, please, and as many other curry accompaniments as are handy: crisp, crushed bacon, coarsely chopped nuts, Indian relish, grated coconut, chopped hard-cooked eggs, green onion, green pepper. . . .

It's easy to cook like gourmet though you are a beginner. We want you to believe just as we do that in this miraculous age it is quite possible—and it's fun—to be a "chef" even before you can really cook. . . .

Every recipe includes a short cut—a canned or quick frozen food, a mix or a new and simplified way to arrive at a particularly detectable result. . . .

A chef does not serve a dish, he *presents* it and his presentation is every bit as important as his preparation. Much of the difference between just cooking and epicurean cooking is the *difference in the way the food is served.* In our effort to lift quickly prepared food to extraordinary heights of appeal we have appended to each recipe a few lines titled "At serving time," which tell you how to serve, how to garnish attractively and with originality, and, in many cases, what to serve with each particular food for an interesting, well-balanced meal. . . .

Wine is very helpful in glamorizing simple dishes and simple meals, but here too, it is wise to be cautious as to the amounts used and careful also as to the quality. When improvising your own recipes, add half as much wine as you think you'll need. Taste frequently as you add to be sure the wine will not overpower all other flavors. . . .

In a number of instances we have suggested the simple drama of serving ordinary foods flambé, or afire. Too many people feel that such theatrics should be confined to the Christmas pudding or an occasional Cherries Jubilee, but a number of famous restaurants have led the procession and now all manner of foods from appetizers through soups, meats, fish, puddings, and ices acquire a new attractiveness as well as a definite mellowing and blending of flavors by the addition of some type of spirits, which we suggest should be lightly warmed before being set afire.

31

Revolution in the Kitchen
February 15, 1957

In this interview with U.S. News and World Report, *William B. Murphy, president of Campbell's Soup, describes reasons for an optimistic sales outlook for TV dinners and other prepackaged convenience foods.*

Q: What is the trend as to time spent in the kitchen by the housewife?

A: The trend is down. Thirty years ago, the average housewife had to spend five to six hours of her day in the kitchen preparing meals. Today she spends less than half that time. That reduction is primarily due to her use of foods which are partially or fully prepared for her—foods that have built-in services. For example, bread, cake mixes, canned fruits and vegetables, canned soups, frozen foods of all kinds, baby foods, packaged dairy products, precut and prepared meals, prepared desserts including ice cream.

From "Revolution in the Kitchen," *U.S. News and World Report*, February 15, 1957, 56, 60, 63.

Q: What has brought about this trend?

A: I suppose the last war had a lot to do with bringing about this trend. Also, it's the result of aggressive action by the food industry and the change in the attitude and, in some cases, the occupation of the housewife. A lesser but important factor is the scarcity of servants. Of course, many more women are working today—30 per cent of all women of working age as against 16 per cent in 1940. The working woman has less time for kitchen work.

An interesting thing has happened. There's an economic law, called Engel's law, which says: As family income increases, the percentage of money for education, travel and recreation goes up; the percentage for housing and utilities is unchanged and the percentage for food goes down. But, since the last war, this law hasn't worked.

Since 1950, for example, the food percentage has gone up from 22 to 25 per cent of family income. That's because there is built-in service in the foods today and people are buying a greater variety of foods that are convenient to serve. The work in the kitchen has lessened. It's a kind of revolution in the kitchen. . . .

Q: What's going on in the kitchen itself—the revolution within the kitchen—is there one other than in foods?

A: Well, the so-called revolution in foods has caused a revolution in the kitchen. It means that food is being prepared before it reaches the kitchen. . . .

Q: What is left for the kitchen, then?

A: The kitchen is the point for assembling the menu, for the preparation of some foods, for the heating and serving of prepared foods. There's lots of room for imagination in the serving of prepared foods. For example, in the case of our products, canned soups may be mixed for new combinations, they can be used as sauces and they serve as ingredients. Also, the ingenious housewife can enhance them with croutons, with whipped cream, with her own special added ingredients.

Then, there are some foods that will always lend themselves to being homemade—a good *soufflé*, for example, or the just-right omelette, or the lamb chop cooked exactly right, and there is plenty of skill required to make a good cup of coffee.

The housewife has her hands full doing a topnotch job without bothering with the paring, the kneading, the long hours of stirring and the big loads of pots and pans required for full-scale home cooking.

Q: Do you see the trend toward more and more packaged meals, so that a housewife could come in in the morning and pick off a package labeled "breakfast"?

A: There may be some of that, but there is too much desire for individual choice. I think there will be a big increase in what you might call a packaged course or a packaged dish. For example, to have a prepared meat loaf in a form to serve, say, two people, or a dish of haddock with the sauce on it, all you have to do is heat it—instead of the housewife's going to the store, making sure the fish is fresh and doing all of the preparatory work.

Q: Do people really go for those prepared "TV dinners"?

A: We sell quite a few of them.

Q: Are they increasing?

A: Sales are up, I think, 50 or 60 per cent over a year ago, and our business in canned soups, which is one of the oldest prepared foods, and our other prepared foods has more than doubled in the past 10 years. . . .

Q: Why do people want things so highly packaged?

A: To save trouble. The average housewife isn't interested is making a slave of herself. When you do it day after day after day, it tends to get a little tiresome, and the young housewife is really less interested in her reputation as a home cook today. She used to feel it was her duty to do all this homework, and she's lost some of that. She's interested in nutrition, in food values, and in her family's health and happiness. She doesn't regard slaving in the kitchen as an essential of a good wife and mother. She'll slave if necessary, but not if someone else will do the hard work and deliver value.

32

PEG BRACKEN

The I Hate to Cook Book
1960

*Even as married women entered the paid labor force in increasing num-
bers, observers and marketers retained traditional assumptions about
all women's priorities as mothers and homemakers. These assumptions
were never universal, of course, even among the population of white
middle-class women who were most able to remain at home. The burden
of cooking, in particular, came under humorous attack from author Peg
Bracken, who poked fun at the era's domestic ideology even while embrac-
ing some of its basic tenets. Her wisecracking cookbook,* The I Hate to
Cook Book, *sold more than three million copies.*

Introduction

Some women, it is said, like to cook.

This book is not for them.

This book is for those of us who hate to, who have learned, through
hard experience, that some activities become no less painful through
repetition: childbearing, paying taxes, cooking. This book is for those
of us who want to fold our big dishwater hands around a dry Martini
instead of a wet flounder, come the end of a long day.

When you hate to cook, life is full of jolts: for instance, those ubiquitous full-color double-page spreads picturing what to serve on those
little evenings when you want to take it easy. You're flabbergasted. You
wouldn't cook that much food for a combination Thanksgiving and Irish
wake. (Equally discouraging is the way the china always matches the
food. You wonder what you're doing wrong; because whether you're
serving fried oysters or baked beans, your plates always have the same
old blue rims.)

And you're flattened by articles that begin "Of course you know that
basil and tomatoes are soulmates, but *did* you know . . ." They can stop

From Peg Bracken, *The I Hate to Cook Book* (New York: Harcourt, Brace, 1960), ix–xii,
3–8.

right there, because the fact is you didn't know any such thing. It is a still sadder fact that, having been told, you won't remember. When you hate to cook, your mind doesn't retain items of this nature. . . .

Not only are there pleasanter ways to shorten your life, but, more important, your husband won't take you out for enchiladas if he knows he can get good enchiladas at home. . . .

Now, about this book: its genesis was a luncheon with several good friends, all of whom hate to cook but have to. At that time, we were all unusually bored with what we had been cooking and, therefore, eating. For variety's sake, we decided to pool our ignorance, tell each other our shabby little secrets and toss into the pot the recipes we swear by instead of at. . . .

These recipes have not been tested by experts. That is why they are valuable. Experts in their sunny spotless test kitchens can make anything taste good. But even we can make these taste good. . . .

30 Day-by-Day Entrees

OR THE ROCK PILE

Never doubt it, there's a long, long trail a-winding, when you hate to cook. And never compute the number of meals you have to cook and set before the shining little faces of your loved ones in the course of a lifetime. This only staggers the imagination and raises the blood pressure. The way to face the future is to take it as Alcoholics Anonymous does: one day at a time.

This chapter contains recipes for thirty everyday main dishes. Some of them aren't very exciting. In fact, some are pretty dull. . . .

The thing about these recipes is this: they're *here!* You don't have to ferret them out of your huge, jolly, encyclopedic cookbook. *And they'll get you through the month!*

After all, who needs more than thirty recipes? You already have your own standard routines: the steak-roast-and-chop bit, the frozen-TV-dinner bit, the doctored-up-canned-beans bit, not to mention your mother's favorite recipe for Carrot-Tapioca-Meat Loaf Surprise. And if somebody waves a dinner invitation, you leap like a trout to the fly. So, with these additional thirty, you're in. . . .

SWEEP STEAK

4–6 servings

(So-called because a couple of seasons ago this recipe swept the country.)
    2- to 3-pound round steak or pot roast
    package of onion soup mix
Put the meat on a sheet of aluminum foil big enough to wrap it in. Sprinkle the onion-soup mix on top of it, fold the foil, airtight, around it, put it in a baking pan, and bake it at 300° for three hours or 200° for nine hours, it really doesn't matter. You can open it up, if you like, an hour or so before it's done, and surround it with potatoes and carrots.

Socialist Kitchens

33

MARIA OVSYANNIKOVA

The Woman in Soviet Life

March 1959

Inaugurated in 1956, USSR *was a brightly illustrated English-language magazine published by the Soviet Embassy in the United States. It was designed to acquaint Americans with Soviet society, industry, science, and culture. The author of this article served on the Women's Committee of the Presidium, the chief policymaking body of the Soviet Union, and edited the journal* Soviet Woman, *a publication of the Central Council of Trade Unions that promoted the idea of equal rights for women. Here the author sketches a rosy portrait of Soviet women for an American audience.*

From Maria Ovsyannikova, "The Woman in Soviet Life," *USSR*, March 1959, 20–21.

There is no area of national effort to which Soviet women have not made their contribution. Some months ago we were host to Mrs. Eaton, wife of the Cleveland industrialist.[1] Mrs. Eaton told us she had been deeply impressed with the large and creative role that Soviet women play in all spheres of the country's life. "I grew fond of many of them," she said, "and I am going to tell the women at home about them."

Women's role in Soviet life is really many-faceted. We can find women holding down almost every kind of job, even those which were once considered man's special domain. However, our labor laws are very rigid and no management is allowed to employ women on jobs which might endanger their health. As for all other types of work, women have the same opportunity as men and they get equal pay for equal work. At the same time labor legislation gives them certain privileges safeguarding their specific interests. . . .

One of the questions our foreign visitors frequently ask is why the majority of Soviet women work. Do they have to?

Maria Materikova, a worker in a spinning and weaving mill in Leningrad, answered the question this way: "What's so unusual about the fact that so many of us prefer to work? I'd be miserably bored and unhappy without this feeling I have that I'm useful, that I'm part of a big group of people working together, that my work is contributing something to building the country and to raising living standards for everybody. I can't imagine myself without social work, even for a short time."

Many Soviet women do not find housework and a family enough of a career by itself. In answer to the question of a French visitor who wanted to know whether she would leave her job when her second child was born—she was on maternity leave then—Engineer Anna Kovalenko, assistant superintendent of the heat-treating shop in the Kharkov Tractor Plant, answered: "There is a creative satisfaction I get from my job. As much as I like raising a family I find it hard to think of it as a full time job that would take all my interest and attention. I think that a job, far from interfering with family duties and responsibilities, makes for a happier and fuller family relationship. A woman then is not only a wife but also her husband's comrade."

A great deal is being done in our country to free women from household chores and simplify the problem of caring for children. The

---

[1] Joseph E. Eaton founded the Eaton Manufacturing Company, which produced automotive parts. The Soviets often sought technological and executive advice from American industrialists.

number of nurseries and kindergartens have steadily increased, and more boarding schools are being opened all the time. The numbers of public catering, laundering and other such work-reducing enterprises are rapidly growing to give women not only the right but the real possibility of a career outside the home.

34

R. PODOL'NYI

Technology on the March

1959

This editorial essay appeared in a Russian magazine addressed to women, Sem'ia i shkola *("Family and School"). As part of a longer piece on the need to expand technical education for Soviet schoolchildren, this excerpt suggested that the increasing penetration of advanced technology into housework and other parts of everyday life was a defining and triumphant achievement of modern socialism.*

The Engineering of Housework

Vladimir Ilych Lenin dreamed of a time when "electrical lighting and heating would rescue millions of 'household slave-women' from the need to waste three quarters of their lives in a stinking kitchen."

This time is coming. The mechanization and electrification of housework are sweeping into the household's every corner. Kitchen appliances have been created that peel potatoes and other vegetables as well as slice them, that beat eggs and grind coffee, and that perform dozens of other minor, but labor-intensive functions. These appliances are brought together in food processors, our so-called "kitchen combines." The very use of these latter two words together seems strange and provokes a smile. But the "universal kitchen machine" certainly lives up to its name. The "UKM" food processor released by Moscow

From R. Podol'nyi, "Teknika nastaupaet," *Sem'ia i shkola* 12 (1959): 9–11. Translated by Charles Byrd.

factories consists of meat grinder, juicer, vegetable-slicer, potato-peeler, and dough-mixer all operated by a single electronic drive. This combo is easy to use, but quite complex in its construction.

Technology in the kitchen significantly reduces the expenditure of time on household chores. Dishwashing machines are neither the first nor the last word in technology, but already they cut by 50% the time spent by a housewife washing dishes by hand for a family of four to six, about 600 hours per year. Everyone is acquainted with vacuum cleaners and washing machines. Today's agenda includes the widespread production of air-conditioners and their installation for use in everyday life. These artificial-climate machines suck air out of an apartment, replacing it with outside air cleansed of dust and heated or cooled to the necessary temperature and previously specified humidity. The release of a series of these appliances has already been scheduled for one of Azerbaidjan's machine-building factories. . . .

It would be possible to name many other technological devices of considerable value to the homemaker. Far from all of these have as yet taken over the functions rightfully theirs, but the current pace of the development and distribution of technology is certainly rapid. In popular magazines from the early 1930s one can find science-fiction stories about . . . television. But within two or three decades television became not only a reality, but part of everyday life.

Each triumph of technology makes new demands of humankind, and not only in factories. At home a man or woman increasingly turns out to be the sole operator and adjuster of many different mechanisms. Their functioning will soon be regulated by photo-electronic relays, timers, and perhaps small computers. Housework will no longer be conducted "by hand." It will be "managed."

35

MARIETTA SHAGINIAN

Reflections on the American Exhibition

August 23, 1959

Published in an official newspaper of the Soviet government a month after Richard Nixon's visit to Moscow, this piece by critically acclaimed poet, novelist, and nonfiction writer Marietta Shaginian elaborated on Khrushchev's critique of Nixon's "capitalist attitude toward women" (see Document 5).

Having entered with my reader the American Exhibition in Moscow just before its recent closing, I, too, would like to take up the study of facts. Only facts and honest analysis of them can demonstrate to the organizers of the exhibition what was interesting to our people, what was not, and what it seems to us was the basic miscalculation of the exhibition, a fundamental error which could easily have been corrected. . . .

The organizers of the exhibition have expended a great deal of work and energy to acquaint us with the way of life of the "average American" and some of what is exhibited is truly interesting. Very good are the articles of everyday life (dishes, pots, tools for the cleaning and preparation of food, machines for the quick freezing of produce, an exemplary kitchen, furniture, a small home). Perhaps what pleases me most of all among these exhibits was a convenient garbage disposal system which uses electric knives to grind garbage into tiny pieces which are then sent down the plumbing pipes.

But way of life is a very individual thing: Each nation, each social system has its own tastes and ideals in this regard. The electronic kitchen which the Americans promise for the future, for example, appears to us very convenient for public cafeterias and large restaurants, but cumbersome in personal everyday life. The countless everyday conveniences of the Americans forever consolidate, as it were, the mission of woman as household manager, as wife and as cook. They lighten the burden

From Marietta Shaginian, "Razmyshleniia na amerikanskoi vystavke," *Izvestia*, August 23, 1959, 5. Translated by Charles Byrd.

of this role, but this very process of lightening the load of individual domestic life perpetuates this role for woman as a profession. But we like new developments that actually emancipate women: new types of buildings with a large shared kitchen for all inhabitants, that is to say, with a cafeteria; with a laundry-room where gigantic machines do all the laundry, not just for a single family. . . . And here the tastes and involuntary expectations, sometimes even unclear to oneself, of the viewer and the organizers of the exhibition part ways.

A truly gargantuan load of abundant items for personal use comes to weigh on the visitor to the exhibition, as if in demonstration of the power of things over man. But the organizers of the exhibition naively think that our Soviet viewer will be consumed by a thirst for ownership of such private property. From the fact that visitors to the exhibition energetically grab up commemorative pins (incidentally, on that very day losing them or forgetting about them) the Director of the U.S. Information Agency, Mr. Allen, recently drew the following conclusion: "Perhaps what expresses itself is not merely a passion for souvenirs. In a country where almost all property belongs to the government, material objects which can be considered one's very own exercise a particular fascination."

This conclusion (made at a presentation at the National Press Club on August 13) is so unexpected that one does not even feel like laughing at it. My God, can it really be that in a country we know and love from an abundance of books so little is known about our Soviet government, ruling one-sixth of the Earth's terrestrial surface? Indeed, here it is fitting not to laugh, but to cry. Observe, Mr. Allen, our life the way we observe yours. Indeed, that which you call "government property" belongs in our country to all people, while your little word "almost" in no way corresponds to all that we may possess as individual property, beginning with weekend and vacation cottages, grand pianos, automobiles, book collections and ending with those very washing machines and refrigerators. And not quite enough of these last items precisely because production cannot keep up with demand.

What the Americans have that interests us is technology, which, by the way, the exhibition did not show us. The cosmetic exercises in the pavilion of Elena Rubinstein are conducted to make women's faces look stupid (if I many speak honestly), smothered in makeup. And here booklets devoted to fashion—in which the most important thing should be the sewing pattern—are given to visitors without sewing patterns, although in America every year one hundred million of such home sewing patterns are published. The technology of cutting, the technology for the construction of housing, the technology for sanitary packaging, the technology for apartment ventilation, for ozone generators and so on and so on—all of this, important as it is, for the individual's and society's everyday life, has been better worked out in America than in our country. Here we can and want to learn a great deal.

But in the area of technology we did not get even a momentary spark of anything that would be useful or instructive at the American Exhibition. The electronic RAMAC machine[1] will answer all your questions about America except for the most simple of all questions: "How?" But indeed friendship and exchange begin with mutual enrichment, and if Mr. Allen would only find time to go to an exhibition of our people's achievements he would get exhaustive, friendly answers to each of his "how" questions.

---

[1] IBM's RAMAC 305 computer was preprogrammed to answer fairgoers' questions with positive statements about American society and politics.

36

I. LUCHKOVA AND A. SIKACHEV

Is There a Science of the Home?

October 1964

The popular Soviet science magazine Nauka i zhizn' *("Science and Life") published this article by two architects who suggested parallels between the unpaid labor of the "housewife" and the paid tasks of factory workers, the heroic figures of communist ideology. The accepted practice of translating the Russian "домашняя хозяйка" as "housewife" has been followed in this excerpt, but the Russian term connotes in English something more akin to "household manager." Unlike the English term, the Russian phrase makes no direct reference to marital status and can be applied interchangeably to a single, divorced, or married woman.*

From I. Luchkova and A. Sikachev, "Sushchestvuet li nauka o zhil'e?" *Nauka i zhizn'* 10 (1964): 22–26. Translated by Charles Byrd.

Modern industry is based on the scientific organization of the processes of production. The rational arrangement of equipment and the organization of the space occupied by every worker are intended to economize the time required for the manufacturing of industrial goods, that is, to minimize the expenditure of labor necessary for each unit of production.

The home is a peculiar sort of factory shop which has its own specific "processes of production." The organization of leisure time, sleep, household chores, the preparation and consumption of food, and the cleaning of the accommodations all demand specific efforts. The organization of the home is intended to minimize the expenditure of labor in everyday life and to free up more time for relaxation.

The basic unit of modern society is the family. To it corresponds the primary cell of living space: the apartment. In addition to residential housing itself, the complex of living space includes day-care centers and kindergartens, schools, commercial enterprises and community-service institutions.

The growth of social services derives from efforts to increase the productivity of everyday labor on the basis of the division of labor. This is possible only through the widespread implementation of machines. Technology increasingly penetrates everyday life. The refrigerator and the television, the vacuum cleaner and the washing machine have significantly influenced the entire character of the home.

The mechanization of everyday life is occurring in two directions: the substitution of machine labor for work by hand inside the apartment and the displacement of certain activities outside the boundaries of the home, that is to say, into the sphere of social services.

The washing machine brings great relief to the housewife. However, doing laundry at home is less efficient than at an outside facility, where it is possible to install more powerful machines and more rationally organize the whole process of doing laundry. The expansion of various kinds of communal services influences the organization of the home apartment itself. And so, the development of communal nutrition will lead to a diminished role for the apartment kitchen. The apartment kitchen will be transformed into a final prep room for partially prepared food, and in the future will almost completely die out. . . .

Work in the kitchen is, in essence, a process of production that still remains within the boundaries of the apartment. Carefully researching the actions of the housewife in the kitchen, it is possible to observe that in different kitchens the exact same work requires different quantities of time and energy.

The kitchen is outfitted with stove, table, sink, cupboards and refrigerator. During her time in the kitchen the housewife moves among these objects. And her journey is not such a short one. Within a single twenty-four-hour period, a housewife may traverse as many as 10–12 kilometers. It is possible to shorten this journey by correct placement of fixtures and appliances.

Much research has been conducted showing that it is most often necessary to move between stove, table and sink. It is therefore advisable to place these things as close to one another as possible.

It has already become a rule in all modern kitchens that the stove, table, and sink compose a single unit. The sideboards have entirely been forced out by hanging cabinets which do not require additional floor space. . . .

Along with the use of machines, a great role in the economizing of time is being played by the implementation of special finishes for the maintenance of cleanliness which require less labor and time. One of the most labor-intensive chores has always been the scrubbing of the floor. The creation of the electric floor polisher has brought significant relief. However, an even more radical solution has been the use of special lacquer floor coatings which have made both the scrubbing of the floor and the floor polisher obsolete.

4

Down on the Farm

During the 1950s, Nikita Khrushchev was determined to use his recently consolidated power to provide the Soviet people with what they had long awaited: more food, and quickly. He therefore pledged to overtake the United States in the production of meat and milk in just a few years. However optimistic this goal appeared, the pledge was no spontaneous boast. Khrushchev had personally witnessed the recurrent famines in the countryside that resulted from two world wars and from the violent process of forced farm collectivization (though as a loyal Soviet official, he oversaw the collectivization of Ukrainian agriculture and never doubted the necessity for socialist agricultural units). In his rise to the top, Khrushchev had styled himself an agricultural expert, and after Stalin's death in 1953, he made three previously unthinkable admissions: that rural villagers were desperately poor, that collective and state-run farms needed reform, and that Soviet farmers would respond patriotically to what we might today term "market incentives."

It was not simply a matter of superpower rivalry that motivated Khrushchev to select the United States as both its agricultural model and its bitterest rival: The United States was the world's acknowledged farm leader. In what contemporaries labeled an "agricultural revolution," American farm productivity skyrocketed from 1940 to 1960, outpacing growth in every other economic sector. Multiple scientific and technological changes underlay these gains, from genetic innovations in crop and livestock breeding to stepped-up mechanization and increased applications of fertilizer and pesticides. Indeed, one of the more curious actors in the postwar "peaceful competition" between the United States and the USSR was an Iowa farmer and seed distributor named Roswell Garst. Garst managed five thousand acres, and his business success rested on such emblematic technologies as hybrid corn, nitrogen fertilizer, and enriched livestock feed. Ever on the lookout for new markets, Garst ventured to Moscow in 1955, visited with Khrushchev, and sold the Soviets five thousand tons of hybrid seed. Khrushchev well understood the importance of corn, not as a food for human consumption, but as food for livestock. Plentiful feed grain kept Americans amply supplied with meat and dairy products in the 1950s. During Khrushchev's visit to the United States in the month following the American Exhibition, he traveled to the American heartland and visited Garst at his Iowa farm.

U.S. farmers and agricultural officials insisted that the foundation of American abundance was the owner-operated family farm. Property holders could seize on business opportunities and reap the profits from investments in new technology. Khrushchev, however, dismissed the importance of private land ownership; he interpreted American farm success as a result of scaling up in size and employing the latest machines and equipment. The absence of genuine economic incentives, in fact, is one reason why Soviet agriculture never took off as Khrushchev had hoped and why his promises of abundance were left unfulfilled. The "agricultural revolution" was furthermore a mixed blessing within the United States. The technological advantages of scaling up benefitted those farmers most able to expand their operations, placing many smaller and midsize family farms at a disadvantage. While most Americans celebrated the productivity of their country's privately owned farms, a few understood that the independent, owner-operated farms that had resonated so widely as symbols of American democracy were succumbing, in large numbers, to the same technological forces that Khrushchev admired.

37

EDMUND K. FALTERMAYER

Farmer Khrushchev

August 10, 1959

This national news article appeared in the Wall Street Journal *about two weeks after the Kitchen Debate. In it Edmund K. Faltermayer describes the Soviet system of state and collective farms and the recent reforms intended to make these units more productive. While the American journalist aimed for an objective tone, his reader could not help but be persuaded of the Soviet farm system's inferiority—a position at odds with Khrushchev's emphatic endorsement of socialist agriculture (see Document 38).*

KHARKOV, U.S.S.R.—"A rocket is not a cucumber," Nikita Khrushchev recently told a group of farmers.

Mr. K's terse aphorism carried a world of meaning for his Russian audience. For while the U.S.S.R. awed the rest of the world by the way it has organized its scientific manpower for outer space probes and other breathtaking technological achievements, after more than 30 years of intensive economic planning it still hasn't been able to solve its "farm problem."

Since Stalin's death in 1953, to be sure, sizable gains in agricultural production have been made. Grain, the backbone of the Russian diet, reached a record production rate last year of 139.4 million metric tons, compared with only 82.5 million tons in 1953. Sugar beets, potatoes, meat, eggs and milk also are vastly more plentiful than they were in pre-Khrushchev days.

From Edmund K. Faltermayer, "Farmer Khrushchev: He Has Better Luck in Space Race Than with Milk and Meat," *Wall Street Journal*, August 10, 1959, 1.

No Surplus Problems in U.S.S.R.

However, unlike Ezra Taft Benson, whose problems are wrapped up in surpluses,[1] Russian farm planners frantically center all their efforts on producing more. By Western standards, the results are not particularly impressive. It takes about 45 million people—43% of the Russian labor force—to feed a total population of 200 million, while in the U.S. only 8.1 million farmers feed 175 million people. Moreover despite soil banks, acreage controls and other crop limiting schemes, the U.S. farmers grow about twice as much as their Russian counterparts. They fed more grain to livestock last year than the entire "record" Soviet harvest. And U.S. per capita meat consumption, at more than 150 pounds last year, was nearly double the 85-pound Russian average.

This gap between U.S. and Russian agriculture productivity is a matter of prime concern to Mr. Khrushchev, whose early career was spent in the wheat-producing Ukraine and who was called to Moscow in 1949 to take over reorganization of Russia's collective farm system. Significantly, well in advance of his visit to the U.S. next month, Mr. K already has made arrangements to visit Iowa, one of the nation's top farm states, to observe U.S. farm techniques.

Particularly embarrassing to the ideologically minded Russians is the persistence of vestiges of individualism among the workers on Russia's state farms and collectives: An amazing 56% of the Soviet's dairy cows are still individually owned and provide more than half of the nation's milk production. The small private garden plots and poultry and livestock pens, operated in their leisure hours by farm workers, also account for a vital 40% of Russia's total meat supplies and a large portion of its fresh produce.

Even Russia's recent gains on the farm front can be attributed in no small part to the granting of more capitalist-style incentives to farmers. A year ago, for example, Mr. Khrushchev abolished one of the most hated institutions of the Stalin era, the system under which collective farms were required to deliver part of their grain and other crops to the state at exceedingly low prices. This "form of tribute," as Stalin himself called it, enabled the late dictator, by selling bread at a big markup, to

---

[1] Ezra Taft Benson, the secretary of agriculture under President Eisenhower, attempted to decrease farm surpluses and government storage costs by reducing support payments to grain farmers. Benson's policy preferences leaned toward the free market, and his actions provoked deep divisions among American farmers. Benson's critics asserted that he cared little about the fate of midsize family farms and that he overtly favored the largest farm units, which could survive in a low-price environment.

obtain huge amounts of capital to pay for industrialization. Mr. K, in contrast, offered high enough grain prices that farmers willingly boosted deliveries to the state. . . .

Since the mid 1930's, when Stalin liquidated the holdings of the "kulaks," or more prosperous peasants, over 99% of the Soviet peasantry has been enrolled in two types of socialized farms. One is the so-called state farm or "sovkho," in which the land belongs to the state and peasants are paid straight cash wages just as in a factory. The 5,900 state farms today comprise about 27% of the land under cultivation and have about 4 million workers.

The more predominant farms, however, and the ones that have given the regime the most trouble, are the so-called "kolkhozes," or collective farms. There are nearly 80,000 of these and they have about 41 million workers. Theoretically a "voluntary" cooperative, formed by all the peasants in a given village or group of villages, the collective farm belongs "in perpetuity" to all its members and not to the state. Pay, in the form of cash and produce, is determined by the collective itself at the end of the harvest season, and depends on the size of the crops.

40,000-Acre Farms

Smaller than the huge state farms, the collectives average about 5,000 acres under cultivation, not counting woods and pasture land. The state farms average a stupendous 20,000 acres. Many of them are in the "virgin lands" of central Asia where 90 million acres have been put in use in recent years, contributing markedly to Russia's increased grain production. Here, the size of the state farms run as high as 40,000 acres or about 62 square miles.

The state farms supposedly represent a "higher" form of socialized agriculture and are supposed to set a standard of efficiency for the collective farms to emulate.

Despite all the post-Stalin reforms, it is clear there is no real intent on the part of Mr. Khrushchev to retreat to some form of individual farming.

The government, for example, has given peasants on state farms a deadline of two to three years in which to give up their privately owned cows. It also is using "gentle persuasion" on peasants in the collectives to do likewise. So far, there is no national program to compel them to give up their privately raised pigs and poultry and the garden plots themselves.

A Hint of the Future

However, it is no secret that this is part of the eventual scheme of things that government planners envision. In the model collective farm at Kalinovka, the village near Kursk where Mr. Khrushchev was born, the peasants already have "voluntarily" sold their cows and the size of the private gardens is to be reduced in the future from three-quarters of an acre to only three-eighths. And at the "Vladimir Ilich" collective, just west of Moscow, the deputy chairman, David Basilonok, says that "eventually the private plot will be cut down to just trees and a flower garden, so that it will be very pleasant to come home in the evening."

But the process will be a slow one. Even now peasants still get about a third of their total income from their individual gardens. An overnight takeover of these tiny household farms, on a national basis, would court open rebellion in the countryside and almost inevitably would precipitate a serious food shortage in the cities as well.

38

NIKITA KHRUSHCHEV

Speech in Des Moines, Iowa

September 22, 1959

In September 1959, as a capstone to four years of agricultural exchange, Khrushchev stopped in Iowa for two days during his first and only trip to the United States. He toured the campus of Iowa State University, where he viewed its pig farm and a home economics classroom. He also visited Roswell Garst's farm in Coon Rapids, toured a meatpacking plant, and tasted his first hot dog. In this speech before the business leaders of Des Moines, he offered praise for American agricultural methods while criticizing their capitalist operations.

From "Speech By N. S. Khrushchev at the Reception in the Des Moines Chamber of Commerce, September 22, 1959," in *Khrushchev in America* (New York: Crosscurrents Press, 1960), 153–57.

Mr. Mayor, Mr. President of the Chamber of Commerce, ladies and gentlemen, friends.

Allow me to thank you for the invitation to visit your state and its capital, this wonderful city of Des Moines, and for the warm reception extended to my companions and myself.

I am, also, grateful to the president of your Chamber of Commerce and his colleagues for the opportunity I have to address you. . . .

We are happy to visit the state of Iowa, whose fame as a great farming center has spread far beyond the United States.

In the Soviet Union we are aware of the fact that your state holds an important place in the world production of corn and that you have made great progress in dairy farming.

Apparently, you would be interested to learn that one of the biggest agricultural centers of our country, the Krasnodar territory, wants to compete with Iowa in the output of farm products. . . .

The achievements of your farms and the production of corn, meat, milk and other agricultural produce are well-known in many villages of the Kuban valley.

I did not have a chance to visit your country before, but I had many conversations with representatives of the American people and also with our people who had been to America.

I recall, for instance, my talks with Mr. Garst, whom you know, of course, who has visited the Soviet Union on several occasions. . . .

U.S. Economists Are Mistaken

The agriculture of the United States of America and of your state in particular interest us very much.

In the first place, because it is a highly mechanized one, high labor productivity has been achieved on some of your farms through the mechanization of field work as well as of the feeding of all kinds of livestock and poultry. . . .

At the present time your output per person employed in agriculture is, of course, much higher than on our collective farms.

It should be noted, however[,] that some of your economists make a mistake when they mechanically compare the statistics of the agriculture produce on your farms and on our collective farms per person employed.

In doing so, they fail to take into account the fact that in the Soviet Union and in the United States agriculture is based on entirely different foundations.

Whereas your farms are private capitalist enterprises, belonging to individual owners, in the Soviet Union the collective farms represent co-operative public establishments belonging to groups of peasants. . . .

On your farms everything that is economically unprofitable has no right to live and ceases to [exist]: weak farms, which do not have adequate income and working capital, cannot march in-step and live and cannot assure as high a level of mechanization as the big farms.

They fall behind the latter, become ruined and are replaced by stronger ones. The law of competition inherent there operates in your country.

Must Have Large Farms

In contrast to that, in our country, agriculture is developing in different—on socialist principles, and our collective farms represent, as I said, big co-operative establishments, formed through a voluntary association of peasant farmsteads.

Therefore, the number of people employed on such farms does not represent the bare minimum needed to cope with soil cultivation, the tending of crops and breeding of livestock and poultry, but is rather determined by the number of able-bodied persons united by that particular co-operative.

We cannot allow such a situation to arise in which a part of the members of the co-operative would work and some other part would be deprived of that right to work.

We recognize the shortcomings of organization of labor and in the cultivation of labor force in collective farms and are eliminating some of the shortcomings that exist. . . .

It goes without saying that the lag of our agriculture as compared with yours, and I mean in the sphere of mechanization and labor productivity, is a temporary one.

The socialist system of agriculture makes it possible to overcome this lag within a short time, we believe, and attain a labor productivity higher than on your farms.

It overbounds a scope for developing production since it knows of no crisis or competition.

In our country there is no danger of a farm being ruined. We have a sufficient standard of agriculture, skilled personnel, and engineering industry capable of manufacturing machinery needed for agriculture. . . .

We strive to accomplish integrated mechanization of all agriculture production processes by applying more perfect machines, by utilizing in a more practical way the labor force, and thus in insuring a greater output per person employed.

We have very good machine operators in our country, who have already attained a very high degree of labor productivity.

Higher, in fact, than at some of your best farms in cultivating corn, cotton, sugar beet and other crops. . . .

We have a powerful—a great number of tractors and other agriculture machinery. We are now making very good progress, we think, in developing agriculture. . . .

Within a short time, just in five years, the output of grain in our country has risen from 82 million tons, that was in 1953, to 141 million tons in 1958.

The state purchases of grain have increased within these five years from 31 million to 57 million tons.

Within a mere three years we have managed to develop, in the eastern areas of our country, 90 million acres of virgin soil, which is about four times more than the entire cultivated area of Iowa.

Our livestock has also increased greatly.

The amount of ensilage has increased over the five years from 32 million tons to 148 million tons, which included corn, the amount of which has risen from practically nil to more than 108 million tons in 1958. . . .

Within the past five years the cattle farmed in our country has increased by 15 million head; that of hogs by more than 15 million, and of sheep by 30 million head.

This made it possible to increase state purchases of meat to supply the needs of the non-agricultural population of our country.

Within eight months of 1959 the meat purchases were three times larger than in the corresponding period of 1953. The purchases of milk have increased 2.3 times, of eggs 2.2 times, and of wool two times.

We Must Borrow

Our agriculture has great reserves, as I mentioned, and unlimited scope for extending further the area under cultivation, for increasing the fertility of grain crops and developing stock breeding. . . .

Our colleagues and their farmers, who have been to the Soviet Union, say that there is much of interest in our country in the development of science and socialized activity work and in the cultivation of industrial crops and in the development of livestock breeding.

I am sure that your farmers and specialists might have used many of the Soviet Union's achievements both in practical farming and in agricultural science.

You, too, of course, have much that is valuable and instructive to us.

Our specialists who have visited the United States know of your great achievements in corn cultivation, for instance, and poultry breeding.

You have attained the highest meat yield per feed unit in poultry breeding, about one kilogram of meat, approximately, per 2.5 kilograms of feed.

We must borrow your experience. We pay high tribute to the efforts and experience of American farmers, scientists and specialists in agriculture.

Your successes are worthy of high trade and your experience merits study and emulation. . . .

We can learn many useful things from each other, I am sure. I believe I need not talk about the great significance of borrowing each other's experience in the sphere of agriculture and exchanging such experience.

I realize that there are people who are opposed to such contacts and who consider that contacts and also better economic relations between our countries might facilitate, they think, a more rapid economic development of the Soviet Union and successful fulfillment of its plans.

There are newspapers in your country—there are articles published in some of your newspapers, which tried to present our seven-year plan as a kind of a threat, a threat of a Soviet economic offensive, a Soviet economic menace, but the question is, what kind of a menace and to whom can our desire to increase our agricultural production, for instance, be.

What is wrong about our wanting to compete with you, for instance, in the production of corn, meat or milk? Hardly anyone would contend that the consumption of more milk, butter, and meat would make Soviet people aggressive. (*Applause*). . .

Indeed our people have advanced the slogan to overtake and outstrip the United States in all-out products per capita population, but can one see some kind of a menace to Americans in that?

We, for instance, are not inclined to regard the farmers of Iowa as aggressive people on the ground that they are producing now much more corn and meat than the collective farms of the Kuban valley are producing at the present time.

We are challenging you to a competition in the production of meat, milk, butter, consumer goods, machines, steel, coal, oils, so that people should live better.

This competition is more useful than any race in the stockpiling of hydrogen bombs or any other weapons. Let there be more corn and more meat and let there be no hydrogen bombs at all. (*Applause*)

The Problems of Plenty

39

JOHN KENNETH GALBRAITH

Speech on the Farm Problem and the Policy Choices

February 1958

Despite tremendous leaps in agricultural productivity, a "farm problem" existed in postwar America: Agricultural incomes trailed behind national averages, and smaller farms were being overtaken by larger enterprises. John Kenneth Galbraith was not only the most visible liberal economist of his era (see Document 20); he was also trained in agricultural econom- ics. In this speech, delivered before an audience of farmers in Des Moines, Iowa, Galbraith explained why agriculture remained distinct from other economic sectors and why more aggressive government policy would be necessary if Americans wanted family farms to survive.

The Organization of Agriculture

Unlike most industry and unlike most parts of the labor market, agricul- ture is peculiarly incapable of dealing with the problems of expanding output and comparatively inelastic demand. This incapability is inherent in the organization of the industry. Agriculture is an industry of many small units. No individual producer can exercise an appreciable influ- ence on price or on the amount that is sold. As a result, it is not within the power of any individual producer—and since there is no effective organization to this end, it is not within the power of the agricultural industry as a whole—to keep expanding farm output from bringing down prices and incomes. And given the inelasticity of these markets, a large increase in supply can obviously be the cause of great hardship and even demoralization.

From John K. Galbraith, "The Farm Problem and the Policy Choices," in *Problems of the Modern Economy*, ed. Edmund S. Phelps (New York: Norton, 1966), 151–59.

All this, you will say (or some will say), is inevitable. It is the way things should be. This is the free market. This is competition. Perhaps so. But it is a behavior that is more or less peculiar to agriculture. In the last thirty or forty years there have been important technological improvements in the manufacture of automobiles, trucks, and tractors. The moving assembly line, special-purpose machine tools of high speed and efficiency, and automation have all worked a revolution in these industries. Did it lead to a glut on the market and a demoralization of prices? Of course it did not. It did not because the individual companies, very fortunately for them and perhaps also for the economy, were able to control their prices and regulate their output. This is a built-in power; it goes automatically with the fact that there are comparatively few firms in these industries. The steel industry is currently running at some sixty percent of capacity because it cannot sell a larger output at a price which it considers satisfactory. This it accomplishes easily without the slightest fuss or feathers. If farmers had the same market power they could, if necessary, cut hog production back by forty percent in order to defend, say, a $20 price.

The power to protect its market that is enjoyed by the corporation is also enjoyed in considerable measure by the modern union. Early in this century American workers worried, and not without reason, lest the large influx of European migrants would break down their wage scales. They were in somewhat the same position as the farmer watching the effect of a large increase in supply on his prices. But now the unionized worker is reasonably well protected against such competition. Even though the supply of labor may exceed the demand, he doesn't have to worry about his wages being slashed. He, too, has won a considerable measure of security in the market.

Thus it has come about that the farmer belongs to about the only group—certainly his is by far the most important—which is still exposed to the full rigors of the competitive market. Or this would be so in the absence of Government programs. Government price protection, viewed in this light is, or at least could be, only the equivalent of the price security that the modern corporation and the modern trade union have as a matter of course. There is this important peculiarity of the farmer's position. Because of the comparatively small scale of his operations, his large numbers, and the fact that agricultural production is by its nature scattered widely over the face of the country, he can achieve a measure of control over supply and price only with the aid of the Government. . . .

The Choice Confronting Us

It will be plain from the foregoing that expanding output, in the presence of inelastic demand, and in the absence of any internal capacity to temper the effect, can bring exceedingly painful and perhaps even disastrous movements in farm prices and incomes. And not only can it do so but on any reading of recent experience is almost certain to do so. And there is the further possibility that these effects may be sharpened by shrinking demand induced by depression. What should we do? . . .

[I]t seems clear that we must now recognize two separate groups within the category that we are accustomed to call commercial farmers. We must distinguish the case of the very large commercial farm which, there is increasing evidence to show, has been able to return its operators a satisfactory income in recent years from that of the more conventional family enterprise which is in serious trouble. . . .

We hear scholars . . . speak of the need for a further large-scale withdrawal of the human factor from commercial agriculture. But we hear less of the massive reorganization of the farm units which this withdrawal implies. The huge scale of the resulting units is not recognized—or this part of the conclusion is soft pedalled. . . .

For let there be no mistake, an agriculture where the average unit has a capitalization of a half million dollars or upward will be very different, both in its social and economic structure, from the agriculture to which we are accustomed. . . .

Perhaps this development will not be so bad. But we should face up to its full implications. Those who now talk about adjustments and reorganization of commercial agriculture are talking about means without facing up to results. Those who praise the free market and the family in one breath are fooling either themselves or their audience. As I have noted, it is the very large farm, not the traditional family enterprise, which from the evidence has much the greater capacity to survive.

We should also recognize that the adjustment to high capitalization agriculture will not be painless. It will continue to be very painful. And we should spare a thought for the trail of uprooted families and spoiled and unhappy lives which such adjustment involves. . . .

For the Small Commercial Farm

Suppose we do not wish an agriculture of large, highly capitalized units. What is the alternative? The alternative is to have a farm policy in which the smaller commercial farm—what we have long thought of as the ordinary family enterprise—can survive. Given the technological dynamic of agriculture, the nature of its demand and the nature of the market structure, we cannot expect this from the market. It will come only as the result of Government programs that are designed to enable the family enterprise to survive. . . .

Any policy must provide a floor under prices or under income. . . . [A] farm policy that doesn't deal with these matters is like a trade union which doesn't bother about wages. There must be production or marketing controls and these must be strong enough to keep the program from being unreasonably expensive. . . .

The choice today is not the survival of American agriculture, or even its efficiency. The great and growing productivity shows that these are not in jeopardy. What is at stake is the traditional organization of this industry. We are in [the] process of deciding between the traditional family enterprise of modest capitalization and widely dispersed ownership and an agriculture composed of much larger scale, much more impersonal, and much more highly capitalized firms. This is not an absolute choice. We shall have both types of farm enterprises for a long time to come. But a strong farm program will protect the traditional structure. The present trend to the free market will put a substantial premium on the greater survival power of the large enterprise.

My own preference would be to temper efficiency with compassion and to have a farm program that protects the smaller farm. But my purpose tonight is not to persuade you but to suggest the choice.

40

ERWIN D. CANHAM

The Farmer in the Space Age

October 7, 1959

*The U.S. Chamber of Commerce (USCC) represents the interests of busi-
nesses and trade groups in Washington, D.C. In this speech before the
Kansas City branch of the organization, the USCC president celebrated
the accomplishments of American agriculture and declared that the
uncompetitive family farm should be released from government support.*

I am delighted at this opportunity to visit Kansas City in the agricultural
heartland of America. It is true that the relative importance of agriculture in our total economy is decreasing, but there are still many metropolitan areas whose economic well-being depends in large part on farming, on ranching or both. . . .

By now, I am sure you have guessed that I am going to talk about
agriculture, but my speech these days is necessarily composed against
the backdrop of Mr. Nixon's visit to Russia—Mr. Khrushchev's visit to
the United States—and Mr. Eisenhower's scheduled return call on the
Soviet Union.

Much of our attention seems to be focused on the possibility of a
thaw in the cold war. At the moment, it is not possible to evaluate those
visits. Only time will reveal whether a thaw can be expected.

Meanwhile—as perhaps it never has before—the fate of our competitive enterprise system is hinged upon a successful foreign policy. So
too, of course, is the fate of our total society.

Equally important, the vitality and success of foreign policy rest on
our domestic strength, vigor and imagination.

Let me underscore that thought.

The skills and resources under the management and control of American urban and rural business men represent one of the most valuable

From Erwin D. Canham, "The Farmer in the Space Age," address before the Kansas City
Chamber of Commerce, October 7, 1959, Box 21, Series I, Chamber of Commerce of the
United States Records, Hagley Museum and Library Archives, Wilmington, Del.

assets in our contest with the communist power. Let us make sure that we use this asset as fully and effectively as possible.

I think it is significant that Mr. Khrushchev spent some of his precious time in America looking at Iowa corn and hog farms. I also think this was no idle curiosity on his part.

We know that he was incredulous about American agricultural achievements. He wanted to see for himself, because the Soviet Union has a tough farm problem on its worksheet.

As a result of a rapidly growing population, Russia faces a crucial challenge to provide food and fibre for its people. At the same time, the Soviet would like to hoist the general plane of living. But that would mean releasing a part of the farm population for work in other industries.

Perhaps Mr. Khrushchev can find another old Russian proverb to help him work his way out of his dilemma.

Our farm problem is quite different. Our problem is learning how to manage the magnificent abundance which rural industry provides. This abundance is the end-product of partnership between rural business men who work the soil and agribusiness men who supply the farmer with equipment, chemicals and other goods and services.

As a result of this teamwork, we in the United States are the best fed people in the world. It is hardly necessary to document that statement with statistics. All you have to do is to pick up a newspaper and read the latest 10-day diet. There seem to be millions of us who are overfed.

Our supermarkets have forgotten that the calendar is divided into four seasons. Tomatoes, eggplant, melons and little green onions are as readily available in winter as in summer. Turkey is on our tables all the year around. So are lamb and chicken, and our versatile transportation industry is entitled to share in the credit.

Like Russia, we have a rapidly expanding population, but our food industry has met that challenge. The Soviet has far to go.

We might think that because our food industry is imbued with such dynamic vitality that farming would be a prosperous business. I wish it were, but we must recognize the melancholy fact that many of our farmers are not thriving and by no means prosperous.

I do not know the precise number of farmers who fall into that category, but I do know there are enough of them to keep the farm problem perpetually in front of us as one of the thorniest issues of national policy and politics. . . .

The combination of low marginal costs and low marginal prices gives us a coin with two sides: abundant food and fibre at relatively good bargain prices for consumers, but for the farmer, surplus production and unsatisfactory income.

For many years, our federal farm programs have tried to modify this situation by attempting to limit the abundance under the principles of what the economists call the economics of relative scarcity.[1]

This program does not seem to have worked. Nor does it hold much promise for the future. . . .

There are any number of palliative proposals. For example —

In recent years, our attention has been increasingly focused on the idea of using our abundance to help people both here and abroad. We have used a food stamp plan. We have distributed surplus foods to welfare clients and public institutions at low cost. We have inaugurated school lunch and school milk programs. We have sought to dispose of surpluses abroad outside of the normal economic operation of the market. In these ways, we have disbursed at least a little of our embarrassing abundance.

More recently, there has been widespread interest in a sort of permanent program to send some of our abundance overseas. Under such slogans as "Food for Peace" or "Food for Freedom," it is proposed to create additional demands for our commodities that would enhance prices and improve farm income.

On moral, economic and international grounds, such proposals merit our most careful study. From certain quarters, we are told that if we do not use our agricultural abundance to relieve poverty and provide economic incentive to less privileged countries, Soviet Russia and possibly other communist countries will attempt to engage in counter-action programs to make political capital to our disadvantage.

I would like to point out that in spite of whatever merit there may be to this argument, it is essentially negative. If there is moral excellence and sound international policy in the idea of using our abundance to help others, we ought to embrace it wholeheartedly for positive reasons as a worthwhile end in itself. We ought not back into such a program half-heartedly merely in order to pre-empt the field before the communist beat us to it. . . .

---

[1] The federal farm programs that began in the 1930s, during the New Deal, had initially operated as surplus-clearing mechanisms. However, given the yield-boosting effects of the postwar "agricultural revolution," this was no longer the case by the 1950s. The government, in other words, did not "limit abundance"; to the contrary, public subsidies encouraged production. Canham is using half-truths and anti–New Deal rhetoric to build political support for free-market agricultural policy.

The advertised objective of most proposed farm programs is to improve farm income. That is understandable. It is more than understandable. It is all right. It is a worthy objective. No responsible person can be opposed to it. Most certainly not the urban business community which looks upon the rural business community as a source of most important customers.

But I do not see how we can achieve the worthwhile objective of increasing farm income by treating farmers as plants in a government hot-house—as if they couldn't stand the rigors of our economic climate.

It is true that the farm environment is spiritually and morally valuable to our national society, but the farmer is not a museum piece. He, too, must go along with the changes which are inevitable in our type of economic order. We may love the self-sufficient family farm, but we cannot endow it in perpetuity. It must rise or fall on its own. . . .

I am not a farmer, nor am I a business man as commonly defined. I like to think back to the days when farm boys and girls hunted for eggs in the mangers and the haymows. But common sense tells me that in today's market, those eggs could not compete with the product of smoothly organized, extensive chicken factories.

I like to think back to the days when the hired man directed the first squirts of milk from every cow to the outstretched tongues of all the barn cats. But common sense tells me that milk produced in that environment could not compete with the product of modern dairy farms.

Right now, there is a struggle going on between nostalgia and progress.

A migration from the farm is inevitable. Whether this exodus will prove to be rewarding or frustrating depends in part on the farm people involved. At one and the same time, it is your problem and my problem and the problem of all Americans who are interested in creating for the future a nation of such strength and stability that we will continue to grow and be able to provide opportunity for all of us and each of us to realize our best.

41

ORVILLE FREEMAN

Memo to the President re Tour of the Soviet Union

July 30, 1963

Despite moments of high drama in U.S.-Soviet relations, most notably the 1962 Cuban missile crisis, the farm productivity battle continued to structure Khrushchev's domestic priorities and American foreign relations. In fact, an American agricultural delegation headed by U.S. Secretary of Agriculture Orville L. Freeman traveled to the Soviet Union in the summer of 1963. This memo to President Kennedy included a transcription of a conversation between Secretary Freeman and Premier Khrushchev.

We have just completed a 16 day tour of the Soviet Union. We visited state and collective farms in widely differing areas, as well as research institutes and plants for the manufacture of farm machinery. I have brought your greetings to groups of farmers and workers on the average of 5 times a day. Radio coverage has been good, and [in] Minsk, last Sunday, I appeared for half an hour of television discussion, in which I was able to get in a plug for American agriculture and our system of private ownership and individual initiative. . . .

I will transmit, as soon as it can be prepared, a detailed report of the two hour conference that our delegation had with Chairman Khrushchev this noon. . . .

The Secretary of Agriculture and members of his official party met with Chairman Kruschev [*sic*] in the Kremlin at 11:00 a.m. Secretary Freeman presented Chairman Khrushchev with an Indian peace pipe made of stone from the Indian quarry at Pipestone, Minn., with the statement

From Orville Freeman, "Memo to the President re Tour of the Soviet Union," Orville Freeman Papers, Box 2, Folder August 1963, John F. Kennedy Library, Boston, Mass.

that he hoped this would be a symbol of lasting peace between the American people and the Russian people. . . .

NSK opened the meeting by saying, "We are happy to greet you here as workers in a most peaceful field, because workers in agriculture give life to the people and the people are having a new life. This is an area that pleases the people, and we are glad for peaceful competition.". . . He went on: "We have had some success in agriculture, but respect the success of other people in agriculture, too. . . . The level of agricultural development in your country is higher than in ours. This is not the result of your political system, but the result of your riches. The bigger capital investment in agriculture. But now we are going to take this priority from you. (Take the first place from you.)" . . .

"We want to place the Americans behind us," said Krushchev [*sic*].

[OLF]: "We welcome that contest. Peaceful production of food and fiber cannot help but be a good thing. I am sure that the Chairman will not consider me disrespectful if I do not agree with every statement he has made. . . . I will only say that we consider the institution of private property a very strong engine to stimulate productivity and I have noted that the Chairman has frequently referred to material incentives in Soviet agriculture. Certainly this is very important. We welcome that contest."

NSK: "That is correct. There is no use to quarrel about it. . . . You correctly said that we stressed material incentives. . . . But we are entering a new era when we will use moral incentives, a new incentive. We believe in the near future that the moral qualities of people will play an increasing role (moral incentive will increase). A human being has a natural need for work, for labor. . . . We also have some experience, good farms, good experimental farms, research institutes. Besides we have world experience, and there are no secrets in these matters. We will have to teach the people. We have world experience at our disposal, especially U.S.A., Germany, Great Britain, Western Europe." . . .

OLF: "We were pleased to observe American agricultural machines here at various places . . . and the engineering (exchanges) taking place. I think this is a very useful exchange of information."

K: "Agreed. We are buying specimens, and they are good machines. We find McCormick and John Deere are good quality machines. I saw these machines. When we visited the U.S., I was in the John Deere plant."

OLF: "I am interested in observing the effect of increasing prices available to collective farms. As Secretary of Agriculture I have fought hard to try to get better prices for American farmers, but the consumer does not always sympathize with that point of view."

K: "The consumers didn't notice it here. We increased the price for producers, but not for consumers, but only on some animal husbandry products to consumers: Only on products on which we had losses. (We did this) in order that they may have profit and in order to stimulate production."

OLF: "Now that collectives make more money, you ought to follow the good free enterprise system and buy more machinery."

K: "Yes."

OLF: "It would seem this would bring increased investment in agriculture in the Soviet Union. Then you will want more machines."

K: "We have quite a few machines but in some areas we are short of skilled machinists. In this respect, Americans have better."

OLF: "We would observe, Mr. Chairman, that the machines for grain crops, according to my associates who have been here before, are very much improved. But animal husbandry and particularly fruits and vegetables, have not made as much progress."

K: "That is correct. This is a weak point. We have to learn much from you in this and we will use your fundamental experience to learn from you in this field."

OLF: "In the U.S.A. there are fewer than eight million working the land. Here there are many more, and I am curious to know how long the Chairman thinks it will be before there will be a similar movement in the Soviet Union."

K: "I think we will have (a similar situation). I think that will depend on mineral fertilizers and machines. The more we have fertilizers and machinery, the less labor will stay in agriculture. I think after ten or fifteen years we will face the problem of decreasing our own sown areas." . . .

OLF: "Sometimes that is tougher than producing more."

K: "Yes, we need fertilizers and capital investment, and your friend Garst tried to convince me of that. Now we have enough money. Now we are going to decrease money for rockets, we are fed up with rockets, we have enough rockets. We are going to (spend more money on) (divert this money to) agriculture."

42

U.S. CENTRAL INTELLIGENCE AGENCY

The Significance of Four Million Tons of U.S. Wheat for Food Consumption in the USSR

October 15, 1963

Abysmal grain harvests in the fall of 1963 put the lie to Khrushchev's repeated predictions of overtaking the United States in agricultural production. Indeed, the threat of famine pushed Soviet officials to request an opportunity to purchase grain from the U.S. government. The sale required U.S. presidential sanction, however, given a 1949 law that prohibited the export of commodities to "any nation threatening national security." The grain sale was eventually approved as a demonstration of the "superiority of free agriculture" and as a way to reduce government-held surpluses. This Central Intelligence Agency statement, requested by the White House, assessed the potential significance of U.S. grain for the internal stability of the Soviet Union and its foreign relations.

Four million tons of wheat is equal to an average of about 140 calories per capita per day in the Soviet Union. This is about 5 percent of the estimated total caloric value of the average Soviet diet. It is equal to some 12 percent of domestic consumption of wheat for food, which has run about thirty-four million tons annually. Any shortages of bread might have disturbing political consequences since bread is such an important element in the diet of the Russian people. The leadership is undoubtedly aware that grain shortages could lead to civil disturbances in the Soviet Union more widespread than those in 1962. It is expected that the imported grain will be especially significant in maintaining urban consumption levels.

The very poor wheat crop of 1963, estimated at about 44 million tons, left the Soviets some 11–13 million tons short of normal production.

From Office of Research and Reports/Central Intelligence Agency, "The Significance of Four Million Tons of U.S. Wheat for Food Consumption in the USSR," October 15, 1963, Theodore Sorensen Papers, Box 28, Folder Wheat, John F. Kennedy Library, Boston, Mass.

Unusual conditions in recent years may have caused the Soviets to draw down their wheat reserves. Although we do not have any direct information on the extent to which these reserves are depleted, the urgency of Soviet purchases suggest that they are presently very low.

To date, the USSR has purchased some 8–9 million tons of wheat and flour from Free World countries. If they purchase four million tons from the U.S., they will probably have enough wheat to meet current basic domestic food requirements and export commitments, and may replenish their reserves to some extent. The Soviets have been net exporters of 4–6 million tons of wheat per year for the past four years, largely to the European Satellites. We believe that unless they obtain wheat in the U.S. the Soviets may find it necessary to reduce wheat exports to the European Satellites, Brazil, India, and Egypt in order to prevent a food shortage in the USSR.

43

U.S. INFORMATION AGENCY

Khrushchev in Wheat Field

August 1964

In 1965, the U.S. Information Agency circulated this iconic image with the caption: "Nikita Khrushchev stands in a sea of wheat during a tour of [Kazakh] farmlands two months before his ouster as first secretary of the Soviet Communist Party." Khrushchev was indeed deposed in October 1964, after a conspiracy led by his rival and successor, Leonid Brezhnev, coerced him into "voluntary" retirement. Though other factors were at work in undermining Khrushchev's leadership, including various foreign policy blunders, widespread domestic discontent over agricultural shortages and high food prices contributed to his fall. In his memoirs, Khrushchev lamented that Soviet officials during and after his reign had failed to deliver on his proposals for agricultural reform and food abundance.

Image 76-1139, Box 59, Series PS-E, RG 306, National Archives II, College Park, Md.

Figure 8. *Khrushchev in Wheat Field*

A Chronology of the Kitchen Debate and Cold War Consumer Politics (1941–1964)

1941 *January* President Franklin Roosevelt tells Congress in his State of the Union Address that "four freedoms," including "freedom from want," would define post–World War II international order.

December United States enters World War II in wake of Japanese attack on Pearl Harbor, Hawaii.

1945 World War II ends, and mistrust sets in between United States and USSR, once wartime allies.

July–August Leaders of victorious countries agree at meeting in Potsdam, Germany, to divide Germany into four zones of occupation; by 1949, Germany formally split into capitalist West and communist East.

1946 President Harry Truman lifts price controls on meat and other consumer goods instituted during the war; Republicans exploit Truman's perceived bungling of the matter to regain Congress for first time since 1930.

1947 Truman announces Truman Doctrine, committing United States to policy of containment.

Republican-led Congress passes Taft-Hartley Act in attempt to limit strength of organized labor.

Soviet Union develops Molotov Plan to create alliance of Eastern European economies tied to Moscow.

1948 Marshall Plan begins, as United States initiates four-year, $13 billion effort to rebuild Western European economies and bolster American trade interests.

June Stalin initiates Berlin Blockade in effort to force United States out of occupied German capital; Truman responds with emergency airlift of food and medical supplies to trapped West Berliners, which lasts until May 1949.

1949 North Atlantic Treaty Organization (NATO) is formed, uniting United States and Western European powers in a military alliance to defend against potential Soviet attacks.

Mao Zedong proclaims victory in Chinese Revolution and announces formation of communist state, People's Republic of China.

August Soviet Union detonates nuclear bomb, ending U.S. monopoly on atomic weapons.

1950 National Security Council produces classified document, NSC-68, outlining plan for indefinite global war against communism.

Joseph R. McCarthy, senator from Wisconsin, begins four-year campaign to root out supposed communist subversives in government, military, education, and media; such anticommunist hysteria contributes to widespread restrictions on civil liberties during Second Red Scare.

June North Korean communist forces invade South Korea, sparking three-year war in which United States and allied forces confront troops, supported by Soviet Union, from communist North Korea and China.

1953 Joseph Stalin, longtime leader of Soviet Union, dies, setting in motion a years-long struggle for power that Nikita Khrushchev ultimately wins.

President Dwight Eisenhower establishes United States Information Agency, designed to sell "American Way" to overseas audiences.

In his first speech as First Secretary of the Communist Party of the Soviet Union, Khrushchev calls for rapid upticks in agricultural and consumer goods production.

1954 The Central Committee of the Communist Party of the Soviet Union, under Khrushchev's leadership, initiates Virgin Lands Campaign to plow up Kazakh and Siberian steppes for grain production.

1955 Soviet agricultural delegation travels to United States to inspect capitalist farming methods; visits Iowa farmer and hybrid seed dealer Roswell Garst.

Warsaw Pact signed, committing Eastern European communist states to mutual defense pact similar to NATO.

1956 *February* Khrushchev, now Soviet premier, delivers "secret speech" to Soviet leaders, condemning the brutality of Stalin's reign.

June   Workers in Poznań, Poland, arise in mass protests against communist government, which responds with violent repression.

November   Soviet armed forces crush Hungarian uprising, sparking outrage in West while consolidating Soviet control in communist Central Europe.

1957   In Leningrad, Khrushchev pledges Soviet Union will overtake United States in per capita output of meat, butter, and milk within a few years.

Soviet Union launches *Sputnik I* satellite into space, instantly arousing American fears of falling behind Soviets in arms race, space exploration, and scientific and technological education.

1958   Khrushchev proposes "Berlin ultimatum," giving Western powers six months to vacate West Berlin and put divided capital into hands of East German communists.

1959   *January*   Nikita Khrushchev announces bold seven-year economic plan intended to boost availability of consumer goods, especially meat and milk, for Soviet citizens.

May   Soviet leaders back down from "Berlin ultimatum," thawing relations slightly with Western powers.

June–July   Soviet National Exhibition staged in New York City, with demonstrations of *Sputnik*, musical and theater productions, and exhibits highlighting Soviet industrial and agricultural productivity.

July   Eisenhower signs into law congressional declaration of Captive Nations Week, announcing that "the enslavement of a substantial part of the world's population by Communist imperialism makes a mockery of the idea of peaceful coexistence between nations."

July–August   U.S. Vice President Richard Nixon visits Soviet Union.

American National Exhibition, site of Kitchen Debate, opens in Moscow's Sokolniki Park.

"Everything for Soviet Man," a Soviet exhibition intended to compete with American display at Sokolniki Park, opens on May Boulevard in Moscow.

September   Khrushchev visits United States.

1960   Worst year for Soviet agricultural production since death of Joseph Stalin, with meat, milk, and butter in short supply.

Nixon selected as Republican presidential candidate; many commentators attribute his success to his performance in Moscow.

1961 East Germany begins construction of Berlin Wall, a physical and highly symbolic barrier between capitalist West Berlin and communist East Berlin.

1962 Food riots break out in Soviet Union in response to doubled prices for meat and butter.

Cuban missile crisis pits President John F. Kennedy against Khrushchev, with tense negotiations barely forestalling onset of nuclear world war.

1963 United States sells Soviet Union several million tons of American grain.

1964 *October*   Khrushchev is deposed, replaced by Leonid Brezhnev.

Questions for Consider

1. What were the U.S. and Soviet motivations for holding the American National Exhibition in Moscow? What messages did U.S. officials hope to convey? How was the American National Exhibition received?

2. Who won the Kitchen Debate? Explain your response.

3. Why were consumer goods important symbols of progress for both Nikita Khrushchev and Richard Nixon?

4. Why do many historians regard the Kitchen Debate as one of the most illustrative events of the cold war?

5. Why did American thinkers in the 1950s believe a "classless" society was developing in the United States?

6. What advantages did Khrushchev hope to gain by engaging in "peaceful competition" with the West in the late 1950s?

7. What were the similarities and differences between the U.S. and Soviet approaches to economic growth?

8. How did the cold war shape the way Americans viewed their own society?

9. What were Soviet and American feminine ideals during the late 1950s and early 1960s? How were they similar, and how did they differ?

10. A wide range of commentators in the United States and the Soviet Union praised how modern kitchens and convenience foods freed women from household labor. Were women as liberated as enthusiasts claimed?

11. What does the Kitchen Debate reveal about the different ways in which communist and capitalist leaders viewed women's role in society?

12. What political and economic philosophy provoked Khrushchev both to emulate and to criticize the American agricultural model?

13. How did agricultural abundance lead to a "problem of plenty" in postwar America? When and why did political debates about farm and food systems arise in the United States? How did those debates contrast with Soviet farm and food concerns?

14. Was the cold war a conflict that could be "won" or "lost"?

Selected Bibliography

COLD WAR POLITICS AND CULTURE

Belmonte, Laura A. *Selling the American Way: U.S. Propaganda and the Cold War.* Philadelphia: University of Pennsylvania Press, 2008.

Caute, David. *The Dancer Defects: The Struggle for Cultural Supremacy during the Cold War.* New York: Oxford University Press, 2005.

Hixson, Walter L. *Parting the Curtain: Propaganda, Culture, and the Cold War, 1945–1961.* New York: St. Martin's Press, 1997.

Khrushchev, Nikita. *Khrushchev in America.* New York: Crosscurrents Press, 1960.

Khrushchev, Sergei, ed. *Memoirs of Nikita Khrushchev.* Vol. 2, *Reformer, 1945–1964.* Translated by George Shriver. University Park: Pennsylvania State University Press, 2006.

Leffler, Melvyn P. *For the Soul of Mankind: The United States, the Soviet Union, and the Cold War.* New York: Hill and Wang, 2007.

Osgood, Kenneth. *Total Cold War: Eisenhower's Secret Propaganda Battle at Home and Abroad.* Lawrence: University Press of Kansas, 2006.

Taubman, William. *Khrushchev: The Man and His Era.* New York: W. W. Norton, 2003.

Taubman, William, Sergei Khrushchev, and Abbott Gleason, eds. *Nikita Khrushchev.* New Haven, Conn.: Yale University Press, 2000.

Von Eschen, Penny M. *Satchmo Blows Up the World: Jazz Ambassadors Play the Cold War.* Cambridge, Mass.: Harvard University Press, 2004.

Whitfield, Stephen J. *The Culture of the Cold War*, 2nd ed. Baltimore, Md.: Johns Hopkins University Press, 1996.

CONSUMERS AND CONSUMPTION

Blaszczyk, Regina L. *American Consumer Society, 1865–2005: From Hearth to HDTV.* Wheeling, Ill.: Harlan Davidson, 2009.

Castillo, Greg. *Cold War on the Home Front: The Soft Power of Midcentury Design.* Minneapolis: University of Minnesota Press, 2010.

Cohen, Lizabeth. *A Consumers' Republic: The Politics of Mass Consumption in Postwar America.* New York: Knopf, 2003.

de Grazia, Victoria. *Irresistible Empire: America's Advance through Twentieth-Century Europe.* Cambridge, Mass.: Harvard University Press, 2005.

Hessler, Julie. *A Social History of Soviet Trade: Trade Policy, Retail Practices, and Consumption, 1917–1953.* Princeton, N.J.: Princeton University Press, 2004.

Jackson, Kenneth T. *Crabgrass Frontier: The Suburbanization of the United States.* New York: Oxford University Press, 1985.

Jacobs, Meg. *Pocketbook Politics: Economic Citizenship in Twentieth-Century America.* Princeton, N.J.: Princeton University Press, 2005.

McGovern, Charles. *Sold American: Consumption and Citizenship, 1890–1945.* Chapel Hill: University of North Carolina Press, 2006.

Nicolaides, Becky M., and Andrew Wiese. *The Suburb Reader.* New York: Routledge, 2006.

Oldenziel, Ruth, and Karin Zachmann, eds. *Cold War Kitchen: Americanization, Technology, and European Users.* Cambridge, Mass.: MIT Press, 2009.

Reid, Susan E. "Cold War in the Kitchen: Gender and De-Stalinization of Consumer Taste in the Soviet Union under Khrushchev." *Slavic Review* 61 (Summer 2002): 211–52.

Spufford, Francis. *Red Plenty: Inside the Fifties' Soviet Union.* London: Faber and Faber, 2010.

FOOD AND AGRICULTURE

Ahlberg, Kristin L. *Transplanting the Great Society: Lyndon Johnson and Food for Peace.* Columbia: University of Missouri Press, 2008.

Avakian, Arlene Voski, and Barbara Haber, eds. *From Betty Crocker to Feminist Food Studies: Critical Perspectives on Women and Food.* Amherst: University of Massachusetts Press, 2005.

Collingham, Lizzie. *The Taste of War: World War II and the Battle for Food.* New York: Penguin Books, 2012.

Conkin, Paul K. *A Revolution Down on the Farm: The Transformation of American Agriculture since 1929.* Lexington: University Press of Kentucky, 2008.

Cullather, Nick. *The Hungry World: America's Cold War Battle against Poverty in Asia.* Cambridge, Mass.: Harvard University Press, 2010.

Hamilton, Shane. *Trucking Country: The Road to America's Wal-Mart Economy.* Princeton, N.J.: Princeton University Press, 2008.

Horowitz, Roger. *Putting Meat on the American Table: Taste, Technology, Transformation.* Baltimore, Md.: Johns Hopkins University Press, 2006.

Hurt, R. Douglas. *Problems of Plenty: The American Farmer in the Twentieth Century.* Chicago: Ivan R. Dee, 2002.

Inness, Sherrie A. *Dinner Roles: American Women and Culinary Culture.* Iowa City: University of Iowa Press, 2001.

Levenstein, Harvey. *Paradox of Plenty: A Social History of Eating in Modern America*. Berkeley: University of California Press, 2003.

Neuhaus, Jessamyn. *Manly Meals and Mom's Home Cooking: Cookbooks and Gender in Modern America*. Baltimore, Md.: Johns Hopkins University Press, 2003.

Shapiro, Laura. *Something from the Oven: Reinventing Dinner in 1950s America*. New York: Penguin Books, 2004.

Volin, Lazar. *A Century of Russian Agriculture: From Alexander II to Khrushchev*. Cambridge, Mass.: Harvard University Press, 1970.

GENDER AND FAMILY

Cobble, Dorothy Sue. *The Other Women's Movement: Workplace Justice and Social Rights in Modern America*. Princeton, N.J.: Princeton University Press, 2004.

Coontz, Stephanie. *A Strange Stirring: The Feminine Mystique and American Women at the Dawn of the 1960s*. New York: Basic Books, 2011.

Cowan, Ruth Schwartz. *More Work for Mother: The Ironies of Household Technologies from the Open Hearth to the Microwave*. New York: Basic Books, 1983.

Deutsch, Tracey. *Building a Housewife's Paradise: Gender, Politics, and American Grocery Stores in the Twentieth Century*. Chapel Hill: University of North Carolina Press, 2010.

Engel, Barbara Alpern. *Women in Russia, 1700–2000*. New York: Cambridge University Press, 2004.

Feldstein, Ruth. *Motherhood in Black and White: Race and Sex in American Liberalism, 1930–1965*. Ithaca, N.Y.: Cornell University Press, 2000.

Harsch, Donna. *Revenge of the Domestic: Women, the Family, and Communism in the German Democratic Republic*. Princeton, N.J.: Princeton University Press, 2007.

Ilič, Melanie, Susan E. Reid, and Lynne Attwood, eds. *Women in the Khrushchev Era*. New York: Palgrave Macmillan, 2004.

Kessler-Harris, Alice. *In Pursuit of Equity: Women, Men, and the Quest for Economic Citizenship in Twentieth-Century America*. New York: Oxford University Press, 2001.

Marling, Karal Ann. *As Seen on TV: The Visual Culture of Everyday Life in the 1950s*. Cambridge, Mass.: Harvard University Press, 1994.

May, Elaine Tyler. *Homeward Bound: American Families in the Cold War Era*. New York: Basic Books, 1988.

Meyerowitz, Joanne. *Not June Cleaver: Women and Gender in Postwar America, 1945–1960*. Philadelphia: Temple University Press, 1994.

Rosen, Ruth. *The World Split Open: How the Modern Women's Movement Changed America*. New York: Penguin, 2000.

Strasser, Susan. *Never Done: A History of American Housework*. New York: Pantheon, 1982.

Acknowledgments (*continued from p. iv*)

Document 5. From *The New York Times*, July 26, 1959, © 1959 The New York Times. All rights reserved. Used by permission and protected by the Copyright Laws of the United States. The printing, copyright, redistribution, or retransmission of this Content without express written permission is prohibited.

Document 6. Ye. Litoshko, "A Talk to the Point," *Pravda*, July 25, 1959, 1–2, translated in *The Current Digest of the Soviet Press*, XI, 30, 1959, pp. 3–4. Copyright © East View Information Services.

Document 7. V. Osipoz, "First Day, First Impressions," *Izvestia*, July 26, 1959, 3, translated in *The Current Digest of the Soviet Press*, XI, 30, 1959, pp. 7–8. Copyright © East View Information Services.

Document 8. Vl. Zhukov, "What the Facts Say," *Pravda*, July 28, 1959, 4, translated in *The Current Digest of the Soviet Press*, XI, 30, 1959, pp. 9–10. Copyright © East View Information Services.

Document 10. LOOK Magazine Photograph Collection, Library of Congress, Prints & Photographs Division, LC-L901A-59-8225–2.

Document 11. LOOK Magazine Photograph Collection, Library of Congress, Prints & Photographs Division, LC-U9-2870.

Document 15. Ye. Litoshko, "'Back Up Words about Peace with Deeds,' Urals Workers Tell U.S. Vice-President," *Pravda*, July 31, 1959, 4, translated in *The Current Digest of the Soviet Press*, XI, 31, 1959, p. 7. Copyright © East View Information Services.

Document 16. Copyright by Bill Mauldin (1959). Courtesy of the Bill Mauldin Estate LLC.

Document 17. Nikita Khrushchev, "Speech in Dnepropetrovsk," *Pravda*, July 30, 1959, 1–2, translated in *The Current Digest of the Soviet Press*, XI, 30, 1959, pp. 13–16. Copyright © East View Information Services.

Document 18. Courtesy of Hagley Museum and Library.

Document 19. John A. Logan, "Modern Food Distribution—Symbol of the American Way of Life," talk before the Boston Conference on Food Distribution, October 20, 1958. Used by permission of the Food Marketing Institute.

Document 20. Excerpt from *The Affluent Society*, 4/e, by John Kenneth Galbraith. Copyright © 1958, 1969, 1976, 1984 by John Kenneth Galbraith. Reprinted by permission of Houghton Mifflin Harcourt Publishing Company. All rights reserved.

Document 21. A 1960 Herblock Cartoon, © The Herb Block Foundation.

Document 23. Nikita Khrushchev, "On Control Figures for Development of the U.S.S.R. National Economy in 1959–1965," *Pravda*, January 28, 1959, translated in *The Current Digest of the Soviet Press*, XI, 2, 1959, pp. 13–19. Copyright © East View Information Services.

Document 24. V. Ye. Semichastny, Speech by Comrade V. Ye. Semichastny, Young Communist League Central Committee, *Pravda*, January 30, 1959, 3, translated in *The Current Digest of the Soviet Press*, XI, 6–7, 1959, pp. 4–5. Copyright © East View Information Services.

Document 25. From "Youth Has Its Say in Love and Marriage," *The Soviet Review*, August 1962. Reproduced with permission of M. E. Sharpe via Copyright Clearance Center.

Document 27. "Goodbye Mammy, Hello Mom," *Ebony*, March 1947. Courtesy Johnson Publishing Company, LLC. All rights reserved.

Document 28. Jean Harris, "You Have 1001 Servants in Your Kitchen," *House Beautiful*, March 1951, pp. 74–77, 150. Reprinted with permission of House Beautiful © 1951.

Document 29. Used by permission of American Standard Brands.

Document 31. "Revolution in the Kitchen," *U.S. News & World Report*, February 15, 1957. Used by permission of Wright's Media.

Document 32. From *The I Hate to Cook Book*, © 1960. Used by permission of Jo Bracken.

Documents 34, 35, and 36. Original translations provided by Charles Byrd.

Document 37. Edmund Faltermayer, "Farmer Khrushchev," *Wall Street Journal*, August 10, 1959. Reproduced with permission of the Dow Jones Company via Copyright Clearance Center.

Document 39. From John Kenneth Galbraith, "The Farm Problem and the Policy Choices," in *Problems of the Modern Economy*, ed. Edmund S. Phelps (New York: Norton, 1966), 151–59. Reprinted by permission of James K. Galbraith.

Document 40. Erwin D. Canham, "The Farmer in the Space Age," address before the Kansas City Chamber of Commerce, October 7, 1959. Courtesy of Hagley Museum and Library.

Index

163